PRAISE AND TESTIMONY FOR
CONVERSATION IS SEXY
AND COACH TODD R. REED

"We all want a great loving relationship. What do we do with them? Coach Todd's passion to share his simple and fun recommendations in 'Conversation is Sexy' will take you and your partner to new levels of love you have always dreamed of."
-Cliff Armstrong, Senior Mentor, Tony Robbins Company

"Coach Todd helped me understand how men think and the meaning behind their actions, and I now have a much better relationship with my husband thanks to this very helpful book."
-Sandra Millen, Chicago, IL

"I learned a lot from Coach Todd on how to treat my significant other better and am trying to keep her emotional tank always on full. This book unlocked so many mysteries for me about women."
-Lloyd Morralis, Austin, TX

"This book was a huge hit at my bachelorette party, when I gave copies as gifts to all who attended. They wanted to stop and read it right then at the party!"
- Eva T. Hare, Orange County, CA

"'I am one excited bride-to-be who can't wait to practice what I learned with the love of my life!"
-Sandy Carlson., Burlington, VT

"My relationship with my wife was at an emotional low, and we both knew it. She gave me 'Conversation is Sexy' and encouraged me to read it. I wanted to get my old relationship back. It's all still a work in progress, but this book helped me to reconnect and better understand my wife. I give it a 10!"
-Richard T., Boston, MA

"I used to get jealous all the time, and it always created a lot of tension in my marriage. This book helped me to look at the jealousy issue in a different way that was actually fun and has en-hanced our marriage immensely!"
-Karen Taylor, Sarasota, FL

"'This book really hit home for me because it gave me the chance to look at my failed marriage and learn from my past mistakes so I won't repeat them It's also given me the tools I need to make sure I keep the lines of communication open with my new man and make sure my relationship remains passionate. I have read a lot of books by so-called experts with lots of degrees, but they always seem to talk down to folks. I loved this book because Coach Todd seems to be just a regular guy who has 'been there,' who aan relate to people,, and who has good info to share."
-Misty Cochran., Charleston, WV

Meet Todd R. Reed
"The Communication Coach"

An award-winning Commercial Television and Radio Broadcaster, Coach Todd Reed has spent nearly 20 years observing and studying human behavior patterns in friendships, dating, marriage, and relationships. His passion is to empower men and women to sharpen their communication skills, understand what makes each other tick, and use conversation to recreate passion and a love *beyond* words.

CONVERSATION IS SEXY (Triple R Publishing, 2011) has created a buzz among couples eager to rekindle the spark that once lit up their romantic world, as well as organizations in search of a dynamic and entertaining speaker.

Coach Todd is a graduate of Montgomery Junior College in Rockville, Maryland, and of Rocky Mountain College in Billings, Montana, where he played tight end for the Battlin' Bears.

Coach Todd is a two-time MBA Television Sportscaster of the Year and a two-time MBA Radio Broadcaster of the Year. In 1996, he was tapped to carry the Olympic torch in the XXVI Olympic Games, held in the U.S. He is also the proud father of six-year-old Raquel Renee Reed.

Coach Todd currently resides in Richmond, Virginia, but travels the world giving keynote speeches, leading seminars and providing consulting/couple coaching services. For more information on these services, visit:

www.conversationissexy.com

CONVERSATION IS SEXY

COMMUNICATE ON A HIGHER LEVEL
CONNECT ON A DEEPER EMOTIONAL LEVEL

BY TODD R. REED
THE COMMUNICATION COACH

Triple R Publishing Company

CONVERSATION IS SEXY
Communicate on a Higher Level
Connect on a Deeper Emotional Level

Published by Triple R Publishing Company

Cover and interior design by A.Ink

ISBN: 978-0-615-40860-6

First Trade Printing: January 2011
Second Trade Printing: February 2011

I dedicate this book to my daughter, Raquel,
who I love with all my heart,
and who means the world to me.

CONTENTS

Why do so many couples struggle to make their relationship work? Why is the divorce rate so high in this country? Why don't I feel connected to my significant other anymore...what went wrong? Will I ever find the perfect woman/man for me? Will I ever be happy in a long-term relationship?

I have asked myself these very questions, and that is what led me to write this book. My goal was simple: to empower men and women to communicate on a higher level and connect with each other on a deeper emotional level. I believe that by successfully accomplishing this goal, relationships will be forever changed.

If you've purchased this book, congratulations on taking a giant step towards building/rebuilding a healthy relationship with your spouse or significant other. CONVERSATION IS SEXY is designed to help you and your partner connect—or reconnect—on a deeper level, both mentally and physically. It focuses on the thought processes and behavioral differences in men and women that can cause couples to misunderstand each other and drift apart. The tips and tools in this book will not only help you pinpoint the strengths and weaknesses in your relationship, but show you how to celebrate those strengths and work on those weaknesses so you prevent them from causing a disconnect.

I love talking to couples I coach about the current status of their relationship. More often than not, they begin with, "I love her, but...." or "I love him, but...." After letting them talk for a few minutes, I will often jump in and say, "If you love him/her, tell me some positive things about your significant other that made you fall in love with him/her in the first place."

What follows are the traits and stories that paved the way for them to become a couple. This is the "gold" of your relationship, and it is these "nuggets" that remind you why your significant other is special to you. There may be traits that are either physical or behavioral that drew you to him/her initially. For instance, your partner may be very romantic or extremely funny and entertaining, or he/she may be very successful in their chosen career. Reconnecting with these fundamental traits can be a great start to focusing on the positive aspects of your relationship.

This book is mainly about communication, the super glue that holds any relationship together. It's a no-brainer that when couples lose the ability to share and express their thoughts, feelings, and emotions, their relationship suffers.

Communication breakdowns happen to the best of us, and while it's tempting to want to point fingers, no one is necessarily to blame. Chalk a lot of it up to the everyday stresses of life—work, finances, raising children—that can wear you down and cause exhausted couples to slowly drift apart. The great juggling act of life can also cause that spark you once had to sputter. Throw differences in the ways men and women communicate into the mix as well, and couples can't help but feel misunderstood...and disconnected.

But what if you could reignite the attraction, passion, and communication you once had? I believe you can and invite you to keep reading for tips, tools, and techniques that will show you how to rediscover the joy and fun of being in a committed relationship.

It is my hope that by reading this book, you will not only learn how to sharpen your couple communication skills, but how to connect--and reconnect--with each other on a daily basis by:

- "Owning" the relationship and working as a team to keep it strong and solid.
- Avoiding routines that can lead to relationship ruts.
- Cracking the gender code to assure that nothing you say or do gets "lost in translation."
- Recognizing the importance of scheduling periodic relationship "check-ups."
- Dodging the pitfalls that can land you in "Communication Jail."
- Learning how to forgive, but not necessarily forget.
- Sharing and supporting each other's hopes dreams—and yes, even fantasies.
- Using nonverbal communication to convey love and affection.
- Learning how to keep the mistakes of your past from clouding your future.

- Pinpointing (and fixing) personal and relationship weaknesses that, over time, can manifest into major intimacy roadblocks.
- Learning how to listen and give constructive criticism based on love—not nagging or complaining. The results will amaze you!
- Clearing the air and moving on when facing conflicts... it's easier than you think!
- Using vulnerability to take your relationship to the next level.
- Using jealousy to your advantage...really!

Once you get back on track, there's a BIG bonus in store for you. Communication can be a powerful aphrodisiac. Yes, CONVERSATION IS SEXY! And in this book, I will not only show you how communication can remove barriers to intimacy, but how, through the simple act of conversation, you can feel the passion and excitement of falling head-over-heels in love...all over again!

I don't claim to be a psychiatrist, psychologist, marriage counselor, or therapist. But I do have 25 years of relationship experience...nearly two decades of professional communication experience spent observing and studying human behavior patterns in friendships, dating, and marriage...thousands of hours spent giving speeches/seminars and coaching couples...a failed marriage from which I learned valuable lessons...plus the love of the most caring woman on earth.

All of this has inspired me to share my wisdom so that you and your spouse, partner, or significant other (terms I will use interchangeably throughout this book to allow you to identify with your own relationship status) can reopen those love lines of communication and rekindle your romance.

Thanks for letting me be your personal com-munication coach! My passion is to empower you and the one you love to strengthen your communication skills, understand what makes each other tick, and use conversation to recreate a love *beyond* words.

Enjoy!

- *Coach Todd R. Reed*

1

"TALK TO ME"

- Conversation is sexy
- Open up to your partner
- No secrets
- Verbalize what you like

Have you ever sat and reflected on the relationships in your life? Perhaps you've wondered, "Was I in the right place at the right time...or in the wrong place at the right time?" "Am I really the good listener I claim to be?" "How often have I held back on expressing my deepest feelings because doing so made me feel uncomfortable or vulnerable?"

Prior to writing this book, I did a lot of contemplating about life and love, and one of my major "light bulb" moments led me to the realization that during my middle school, high school, and college education, I was never taught how to succeed in relationships. As a result, I stumbled—more than a few times—and I suspect you have, too.

● ●

Isn't it amazing the amount of time we spend in school learning about science, math, social studies, health, English and more; yet, we are never taught how to deal with, or really understand, the opposite sex? That's dumfounding, considering that sex (and money) are the two most common causes of divorce in America! Sure, sex education may have been an option—in classes always separated by gender—but information on how to communicate with the opposite sex was never part of the curriculum. Instead, most of what we learned came from personal experience or from watching our friends fumble their way through adolescent relationships.

● ●

Understanding the opposite sex is a difficult task, and most folks are left to learn from little more than trial-and-error (often with disastrous results). Until now! Think of this book as your long overdue crash course in "Romance 101," because when it comes to relationships, I have some tips and tools I believe can drastically improve yours.

● ●

Let's be clear up front. I'm not a doctor, I'm not a psychiatrist, nor am I a psychologist or even a counselor. What I am is a Communication Coach. I have spent nearly two decades in the field of professional communications observing and studying human behavior patterns in friendships, dating, and marriage. I've given hundreds of speeches/seminars and coached numerous couples interested in revving up their relationships by sharpening their communication skills. I also have over 25 years of relationship experience. I've dated younger women, older women, women interested in getting married, and women who just wanted to have a good time. I've made plenty of mistakes, learned from them all, and I hope you can benefit from my experiences.

● ●

Let's begin by diving into some of the major reasons why women and men experience problems when it comes to communication. I encourage you to read this section, reread it, and then reread it again. The concept of communicating with your significant other shouldn't be strange to you. We all talk to each other and chat about what's happening during our day, what we want to do over the weekend, or even what our plans are for next week. But how often do you truly open up to your partner?

One quick and easy way to grade yourself on how well you communicate with your spouse is to evaluate how you express your thoughts and feelings about him or her to *others*. When talking to your closest friends about your significant other, for instance, do you find yourself spilling things to pals that you hesitate to bring up to your partner? Examples:

- "Her meatloaf tastes awful, but she thinks it rocks."
- "He's always ten minutes late, and it drives me crazy."
- "After tucking the kids in, she rarely seems to have time or energy for me, and that hurts."
- "He hardly ever talks to my parents when they call, and that really bugs me."

You know what I'm talking about. Now, grab a pen and paper and take a few minutes to make a list of things *you* say to other people regarding your spouse.

If I made a list based on my past long-term relationship here are some of the things I probably said about my former partner:

- "She doesn't cook enough."
- "It bugs me sometimes that I always have to take out the garbage"
- "Keeping a clean house doesn't seem to be as important to her as it is to me."
- "I wish our love life was more balanced."

My significant other likely moaned to her friends:

- "He's really bad about being on time."
- "He's gets frustrated too easily and is so impatient sometimes."
- "He plays too much golf."
- "I wish he would focus more on what he has vs. what he doesn't have."

When finished, take a look at what you've jotted down. *Every issue that made your list has the potential to grow into a bigger problem and ultimately drive a wedge in your relationship!* Granted, you may wonder how your relationship could go into crisis mode over what you perceive to be relatively small issues like: "My husband leaves his underwear on the floor," or "I get irritated at the lack of effort my spouse turns in when it comes to housework" or "Why do I always have to be the one to empty the dishwasher...feed the dog...cut the grass?" But pick a topic, pick an issue—and if you have conversations with your friends or co-workers about it that include a complaint about your significant other, then there's a problem. And it's just waiting to explode.

•••

Little problems grow into big problems, and undisclosed criticisms you have toward your significant other will eventually affect how you feel about him or her.

•••

I can't emphasize enough that even tiny, seemingly insignificant thoughts, can manifest into negative feelings and cause your relationship to drift apart. Once that process starts, the quality of your relationship may never be the same. Based on my years of communication coaching, I've seen countless couples shut down and stop talking to each other because they were afraid of hurting the other person's feelings. GET A CLUE!

•••

Marriage and committed relationships are the ultimate and highest level of any relationship you can achieve, and I strongly encourage you to use that to your advantage.

•••

In other words, try to remember back to when you first got married or first got together and how much you talked to each other. Recall how safe, comfortable, and wonderful it felt to bring up issues in a loving way and resolve them almost instantly. The goal is to bring back those good old days, and with just a little effort, it can be done.

Now think ahead to the next time you get together with the guys for drinks or enjoy a girls' night out, and everybody starts airing their relationship problems. When the spotlight pans around to you, how cool would it be to find yourself with nothing but positive things to say? Could that happen?

Yes it can, and it can start with you right here and right now. All you need to do is make the commitment that you'll be open and honest with your partner—and in a compassionate way, not in a hurtful or abusive manner. I promise you that taking this simple step will unlock emotional doors you never knew existed and take your relationship to a whole new level.

In fact, when it comes to communication, the bedrock fundamental I've adopted is that CONVERSATION IS SEXY. Have you ever told your significant other, "I love talking to you; I can tell you everything." We've all said it, but do you put the concept into practice each and every day? If not, you're missing a key opportunity to connect with your partner, and when that happens, who knows where it might lead.

Until I met the love of my life three years ago, I thought I was a fairly open guy. I had no trouble expressing a wide range of feelings and emotions—or so I thought. I never realized how much the stresses of day-to-day life affected me. I was all caught up in being a man. I thought I could handle anything and everything life threw my way. Somehow, I had convinced myself that I was "Tarzan" and could handle all of my emotions internally. Boy, was I clueless! I never realized how my emotions and frustrations were building up inside. I was suppressing way too much and not talking about what was on my mind.

What changed? I met a woman who wanted me "naked" emotionally, and who opened the door and invited me to share my thoughts and express my concerns about anything and everything. Being with someone like that (gradually) gave me the confidence to not hold anything back because I might hurt her feelings...and for guys that's huge!

So many men, myself included, will avoid a topic or an entire conversation if we think it's going to stir the pot, cause an argument, or result in an emotional outburst. I refer to this as "Communication Jail." So, not only do my significant other and I talk openly, but she has made it clear that no topic is off limits—and I mean *no* topic.

What a fantastic feeling of freedom I now experience. I want you to enjoy the same!

In other words, opening the love lines of communication is about much more than being able to clear the air by sharing a laundry list of little grievances that are bothering you. Remember, CONVERSATION IS SEXY! Imagine being able to talk to your spouse about *anything*, with no topic off limits:

- How you've had a really bad day because somebody at work said something hurtful or offensive to you.
- How frustrating your financial picture appears.
- How you're not getting the attention from your significant other that you need.
- How adding a few extra pounds recently has you avoiding looking in the mirror.
- How getting a little older really sucks and you're feeling a little insecure about it.

If you're squirming about sharing any of these—or similar—feelings with your significant other, chances are you're male. Study after study has proven that women tend to be more expressive, more open, and more emotionally based then men. When a group of guys gets together in any social setting, I can assure you that they are not likely expressing how great they feel because they opened up and connected with their spouse on an emotional level prior to leaving the house. Guys aren't always an open book and don't talk about how important it is for them to connect on an emotional level.

•••

Posture as much as you wish, gentlemen, and keep portraying that "guy image" around your friends. But remember, if you want a successful and sexy relationship, you need to understand and figure out how to open up to your partner and learn to express yourself verbally.

• •

Okay, so it's not exactly the dominant part of a male's DNA to connect with and share their inner thoughts and feelings. But guys, listen up: Men appear much sexier to women when they're able to open up and communicate their thoughts, hopes, and dreams. And ladies, remember that while men definitely need to work on and develop an awareness that will allow us to express ourselves more often, we need some assistance.

Case in point: Ask us how our day went, and don't be surprised (or hurt) if you receive a one word answer: "Fine." "Okay." "Sucked." Probe a little deeper, though, and specifics will begin to come out. Keep the conversation moving, and before long, you've got a sexy conversation going. I say sexy, because *anytime a couple connects and shows the other how much they care, it's sexy.*

One couple I coached experienced a major shift in their relationship after modifying their dinner routine. When I asked them to describe their environment at dinner, they said that most of the time, they would eat while watching TV, mostly a cable news station. That typically led to a discussion about what was going on in the world, then they would briefly chat about their day. Both described the experience as "enjoyable, but shallow." After we talked about how to create an environment that would not only feel more relaxing, but that promoted more intimate conversation, they agreed to switch up their routine.

Now, when it's time for dinner, the TV gets turned off, and some soothing music gets turned on. Both confessed that, initially, sitting at the table looking at each other felt a bit awkward. They wondered, "What do we talk about?" "How do we deal with this weird sensation?" But, slowly, they began to talk to each other more. They began chatting about the highs and lows of their respective days, and over time, both got more comfortable and began expressing themselves in ways neither had done in years. Sure, politics, finances, and current events came up. But soon, so did discussions about their love life. No topic was off limits! Individually, they began to feel more connected to each other. And it was no surprise to me at all when both reported experiencing a resurgence in their physical love life.

When I asked this couple to describe the change in their routine, the husband was very clear: "In the beginning, it took some getting used to, but I now look forward to the time we spend together at the table. We talk more, and I tell her everything that's on my mind. Being able to do this makes me feel closer than ever to her."

Connecting with your partner by opening up involves a couple of simple ground rules. First, always verbalize your feelings in a calm tone of voice. Otherwise, you set yourself up for confrontation instead of connection. Second, be still and listen to what your spouse is telling you.

Learning to become a better listener pays immediate and enormous dividends in any relationship. For reasons that I can't seem to figure out, the art of listening has become exceedingly less important to many people. Whenever I'm working with an individual or a couple, it never ceases to amaze me how quickly the topic of listening comes up. In 99.9% of the couples I've coached, not listening appears to be at the root of their problems. She might say, "He's always looking for solutions, when I just want him to hear me out." Or, he might say, "She's always accusing me of not listening, when I swear I'm hearing every word she's saying."

Regardless of the reason offered, the result is the same. Its one thing to *hear* what someone is saying to you, and a completely different concept to *listen* to what someone is saying. Listening not only involves absorbing the actual words someone is using to describe how they feel, but taking in the emotions that support those words. Saying "I love you" is a touching thing to say, but it only carries weight if you actually mean it, and the person you are saying it too receives both the words and emotion behind it.

I encourage you to begin working on your listening skills today. The goal is to verbalize your thoughts, as well as to hear and absorb the message your spouse is trying to deliver. But you must be able to focus on the message. Be present in any conversation you have with your spouse, and don't let yourself be distracted by the TV, radio, kids, or a project that you're working on. If you can't multi-task (and guys, you *know* we have trouble with this one), then ask if the conversation can be postponed to a more appropriate time. Trust me, your significant other will appreciate the gesture, knowing that he/she can count on your undivided attention in the not-too-distant future.

When it comes to listening to your significant other, there are some major gender differences you should be aware of. Yep, there's plenty of scientific proof that men and women listen differently. In fact, brain scans reveal that, while listening, men's brains are far more active on the left side than the right side. In women, however, both left and right temporal lobes are activated equally. What does all this mean? Let me break it down for you...

As stated earlier, we men tend to have a lot of trouble multi-tasking. Typically, we can only handle one task—or discuss one topic or problem at a time. So, ladies, please don't throw the kitchen sink at us, or we may just shut down.

Tell us exactly what you're thinking and feeling, too. Tons of studies show that, instead of speaking their minds, women have a tendency to drop hints or make subtle suggestions and expect men to be mind readers. It's not going to happen! If you don't tell us exactly what you mean, what you're feeling, or what you want us to say/do, you're going to feel misunderstood and disappointed. Count on it.

Finally, be aware that guys tend to listen like "statues." We are masters at keeping a poker face, which, unfortunately, leads women to assume that we are bored, not listening, or failing to understand what's being said. Not true! You can blame this one on biology. In their book, *Why Men Don't Listen and Women Can't Read Road Maps*, Barbara and Allan Pease explain it this way: "The objective of the male warrior when listening was to remain impassive so as not to betray his emotions." In other words, our lack of visual emotion enables us to feel in control of a situation—it does not mean we are not listening or experiencing emotions. "In fact, brain scans reveal that men feel emotion as strongly as women do," the Peases acknowledge, "but they avoid showing it."

Guys, there are tricks you can use to improve your listening skills with your significant other as well. The most important one is to recognize her need to talk when she's upset. The most common complaint I get from women is: "He's always trying to jump in and fix my problems instead of just hearing me out." It's true that men tend to be problem-solvers (this appeals to the logical structure of our brains), but when women are concerned or upset about something, it's important to resist that urge to jump in with solutions. What she's really craving is someone to vent to, so be her sounding board instead. Also, acknowledge--both verbally and nonverbally-- what she's saying. Make eye contact, nod your head now and then, and affirm her thoughts by making statements that echo what you're hearing, like: "I can see you're really upset about...." Or "I can tell that......is really bothering you." Simple gestures and statements like these will make her feel heard and understood—and she'll love you for it.

We all enjoy the good times and fun conversations we engage in. But in your quest to be able to talk about anything and everything, surviving as a couple means you'll have to learn how to discuss sensitive and controversial topics in a loving way. Suppose, for instance, that he brings up the topic of how your sex life isn't what it used to be, and you're super sensitive about it. Or, maybe she wants to talk about her perceived lack of support and understanding she feels regarding her job or taking care of the kids, and that's your hot button. When entering into a potentially heated conversation, there are a few ground rules I recommend following:

- Find an object that is small, and use IT to represent having control of the conversation. Whoever holds the object has the floor. Set a time limit to ensure that both of you get to express your thoughts. Take turns making each point.
- Don't interrupt the other person while he/she is talking.
- Don't use terms that are derogatory. Keep profanity out of the conversation.
- If voices begin to rise, postpone the discussion until you're both feeling calmer.
- Take brief notes as the other person is speaking.
- Propose a solution.
- Never, never walk away from an argument and go to sleep angry. At the very least, call a temporary truce or agree to disagree.

I know all of this sounds great in theory, and it's really up to you as a couple to lay out ground rules and guidelines that work for you. Just don't wait for a disagreement to arise before you figure out how the conversation will go and what the guidelines will be. All too often, a slightly heated discussion can turn nasty, and before you know it, both people vacate to different parts of the house just to get away from each other.

What happens next varies from couple to couple, but I want to emphasize that you should be able to talk about *anything* with your spouse. Notice that I didn't say you have to share the same opinion, but you should be able to talk about any given topic. Imagine being a die-hard Republican, and you're involved with a die-hard Democrat. You couldn't be further apart regarding your political beliefs, but the question is: "Can you talk about hot topics without wanting to strangle the other person?" Use the above tools to help you. Agreeing to disagree is a sign of healthy mutual respect—and deep love.

● ●

It's been stated that life can be as simple or complicated as we choose to make it. Choose to run your relationship in a simple manner. This will allow you to experience life with your spouse on a different level.

● ●

In the most blissful relationships, couples talk about everything. Yes, even—and especially—about their sexual desires and fantasies. One of the most memorable couples I coached came to me admitting that they were having problems in the bedroom. Both felt like their sex life was in a rut, but they couldn't pinpoint why their spark had sputtered. Initially, neither was willing to talk in front of the other, so I met with them one-on-one. What I discovered was that she was fantasizing about Brad Pitt, while he was fantasizing about a past girlfriend he'd had a great sexual relationship with. Not that either was interested in actually fulfilling their fantasies, but the disconnect had them both mentally twisted up. Individually, the challenge was to get both to admit that their emotional and sexual needs were not being fulfilled by their partner and put them back on track and focusing on each other.

Have *you* ever fantasized about someone of the opposite sex, either during the day or while making love to your partner? Most people won't admit it, but this is far more common then you think.

In fact, while researching his book, *Who's Been Sleeping in Your Head: The Secret World of Sexual Fantasies*, author and psychologist Brett Kahr surveyed 18,000 people and found that nine out of ten people have sexual fantasies. What's more, he believes that the remaining tenth person has them too, but is too embarrassed to admit it.

Whether you have them or not isn't what's important; what matters is *why* you're fantasizing about someone else. What traits or characteristics does your fantasy lover posses that's lacking in your current relationship?

- Are they sexier than your spouse?
- Are they less inhibited?
- Are they more adventurous?
- Do they push the right buttons?
- Are they more sensual and emotional?
- Do they wear really sexy lingerie?

Fill in the blank and add your own list of qualities that complete your fantasy.

Every quality your fantasy person has relates directly to the issues you're struggling with in your current situation. This can be tough, even embarrassing, to discuss with your partner, and you may need the help of a professional counselor to get everything out in the open. But I can't emphasize enough the importance of taking some time to analyze your list and find a way to communicate these thoughts and concerns to your spouse.

The good news is, once you have this conversation and get everything out in the open, your relationship could go from fizzle to sizzle. That's because studies also reveal that people who fantasize have more fun in bed and have sex more often. So, start the dialogue!

Life gets complicated for hundreds, if not thousands, of reasons, but I know this to be a fact: Your partner has committed himself/herself to you because he/she loves you and wants to enjoy life and be happy. I often say to people:

> *Do you think your better half has dedicated ____ months or years of his/her life so that one day he/she could intentionally screw it all up and cause as much pain as possible?*

Obviously, that was meant to be sarcastic. No relationship is perfect, and some problems are bigger than others. But I want you to know that you can overcome any problem in your relationship if both of you are willing to commit to discussing and resolving any situation or crisis you encounter. This can sometimes be a very difficult and painful process, but in the end, you'll emerge stronger, closer and more connected than ever.

Have you ever been out in public and witnessed an elderly couple walking through the mall holding hands and smiling? Chances are, you've thought about how cute they look or said to yourself, "What a great couple they must be!" Here's what I'd like you to consider when it comes to that couple: Do you have any idea about what problems or heartaches they've had to overcome and deal with in their marriage? Talk to any couple that's survived the test of time, and they'll tell you that the road they've traveled hasn't always been smooth.

If you can learn to open up, talk to your spouse, do away with any secrets, and tell your spouse what you like and don't like, you'll be on a much smoother road to happiness. Be respectful, not confrontational, and remember that it's easy for people to become defensive and shut down. You're looking to establish a two-way highway of open-road communication, and once you reach your "destination," you'll be communicating on a higher level and connecting on a deeper emotional level than you ever dreamed possible.

**CONVERSATION IS SEXY
LOVE COUPON**

"

*I need to whisper
something in
your ear -*

*I promise you
will like it!*

"

2

"ASK WHAT HE/SHE WANTS"

- Learn to give and receive
- Keep turning your partner on
- Be honest about what pleases you
- Talk about fantasies

CONVERSATION IS SEXY because sharing your most intimate and personal thoughts allows you to connect on a soulful, almost spiritual, level with the person you're involved with. At some point in your life, you may have been told that the secret to a successful relationship is communication. But I'll bet that nobody ever explained how complicated that process can be, and how a relationship founded on love, good times, and an emotional bond can—and all too often does—deteriorate, because both people never understood how to talk and express themselves.

• •
Over 250 million people get divorced each year, but the question that no one asks is, "Do you think all those people who got divorced, planned it?""
• •

When I got married, I was 100 percent committed to the relationship and to making it work for the rest of my life. I'm sure most people experience that same thought process when they exchange vows with someone they love. The reality is, I received an amazing education regarding marriage, long-term relationships, and crisis management. My goal is to share that information with you and help make your relationship a success.

As humans, we're not perfect, and the fact is, no relationship is, either. The endorphin rush experienced when we first fall love is one of the most amazing feelings life can ever offer you.

• •
"Ride the wave!" I say. But also understand that every wave eventually crashes and calmly washes up on shore. Enjoy the so-called "honeymoon" phase of your relationship, but acknowledge that the real work is yet to come. Relationships are easy during the dating phase, and even when you first get married. It's two, three, four years into a union when you realize that a committed relationship is beginning to feel a little more like work. That's when the trouble often begins. Learning how to openly communicate early in your relationship, however, can pay huge dividends as you grow and mature as a couple.
• •

The good news is, there are ways to sustain that "honeymoon high" and remain close and connected years into your relationship. One way to accomplish this is to make sure that the giving and receiving in your partnership isn't lopsided.

Here's a potential "light bulb" moment. Everyone likes to be pampered, taken care of, and waited on. But let's face it, most of us like to receive, more than we like to give. How nice is it when your significant other gives you an impromptu neck or back rub? Your muscles relax, it feels so good to be touched, and with each passing moment, you likely experience a major attitude transformation. Ahhhh. Having someone come over to you and put a smile on your face is wonderful. But it's much harder to take that same initiative and spontaneously do the same for your spouse. Instead of relaxing and being in the role of receiver, your hands are doing the massaging, and it takes energy to complete the task. I encourage you to pause and realize what an important task you're engaging in.

• •

Remember, 70 percent of communication is nonverbal and through this physical act, you're actually communicating with your spouse and sending a wonderful and powerful message: "I love you, I'm thinking about you and you're the one I want to be with." You're giving, not receiving, and your spouse knows it.

• •

I can't emphasize enough how important it is to connect with your other half in this manner. It's so easy to fall into patterns and routines. The bad thing is those very patterns and routines can lead us away from intimacy. Lack of intimacy is a dark road that often leads to divorce. I encourage you with every cell in my body to work on being a good giver *and* a good receiver. Take time to do something nice each and every day for your partner, and then watch the love flow.

Another surefire way to sustain that spark that once lit up your romantic world is to have a sexy conversation about...well, sex!

Do you know what turns your partner on? Don't be so quick to answer the question affirmatively. Over the course of any relationship, people grow and evolve, and so do their likes and dislikes. I want to spend a moment talking about likes. As partners, we believe we have a solid understanding of our mate, and that includes what turns them on sexually. As we grow in a relationship, however, our likes and dislikes often change. Whatever got the job done when you were dating, engaged, or even first married, may not be accomplishing the same goal now. Being able to communicate what works for you now—and what may not be working—will help avoid major problems in the future.

• •

Here is the big challenge. Are you able to sit down with your partner and discuss your sex life openly? This includes not becoming defensive if they bring up a behavior they would like to change in your love life. If the answer is, "Yes," then I applaud you. If the answer is, "I'm not quite sure", or even "No," then we have work to do. And there's no time like the present to get started.

• •

What baffles me about men and women is that both sexes have a tendency to air their sexual grievances to friends—and sometimes to anyone who will listen. Imagine a conversation going something like this:

> • *She says:* "Bob just doesn't do it for me anymore. All he wants to do is climb on top of me, take care of business, please himself and fall asleep. When do I get taken care of?"

> • *He says:* "Suzie use to really be adventurous and wild. Now she only wants to have sex in bed, after the kids are asleep, and with the lights off. No lingerie, no Tarzan call of the wild and no variety. What a drag."

While the previous statements were meant to entertain you, they might not be far off base for some couples, and they may even hit home regarding your situation.

• •

Don't let your relationship get to the point where you're talking about your love life to friends or co-workers more than you are with your partner!

• •

Why we do this to ourselves mystifies me, and in the past, I've been guilty myself. It can often be easier to vent or complain about what isn't happening in our love lives to friends—and sometimes even virtual strangers—than it is to communicate those same thoughts to our partner.

How crazy is that? What statement does it make about the status of your relationship when private information is shared with outsiders and not the person you have an intimate relationship with?

One couple I coached learned the hard way that this type of venting or blowing off steam does little more than drive a wedge deeper into your relationship. Both admitted that due to a disconnect in their ability to communicate as a couple, they would occasionally vent to their male and female friends about what wasn't going so well in their relationship. Stan wasn't happy with their level of sexual intimacy, and Kristen wasn't happy with the emotional connection she felt they lacked. Both had legitimate gripes, but instead of discussing their concerns and agreeing on a new plan of action, they shut down and began sharing their complaints with other people.

It should come as no surprise that this process fails at bringing a couple closer together. The reality is, almost no couple is ever 100 percent satisfied in their relationship. But if you're talking/venting to others about what's bugging you—and I'm not talking about issues like your spouse forgot to pick up coffee on his way home last night here—both you and your partner are moving *away* from each other, not getting closer.

So what is the solution? I highly recommend conducting periodic love life check-ups. It may sound silly, but it could help save your relationship—and it worked wonders for Stan and Kristen.

• •

Imagine once a month scheduling a special date night and spending part of that time together talking about how satisfied each person is with their love life.

• •

It's critical that each person have the confidence to say what's on his/her mind and put their feelings out there. I've found in my coaching that while both men and woman want to be loved and fulfilled, what fills up their respective love tanks varies. Men tend to need their physical needs met first and their emotional needs second. On the flip side, women tend to want their emotional tank filled first, then their physical tank. Conducting these scheduled "date nights" allows a couple to get away from the normal stresses of life, relax, connect and talk about what's going great, as well as what may need a little tweaking.

It never ceases to amaze me that, as we go through life, it rarely seems to sink in that little problems are easily dealt with, but larger issues take much more effort, energy, and time to rectify. As humans, we seem to do a pretty good job of letting small problems grow into bigger ones. Open conversation about how you're feeling...open conversation about what's happening in your love life...and most importantly, open conversation about what you'd like to do next is what keeps a relationship healthy and growing.

Ask yourself the following question, and I encourage you to check your ego when doing so: *"Do I really know how to turn my partner on?"* Be as honest as you can in responding. This process of checks and balances can help keep your love life dialed in. One little change here, or little technique alteration there, and everyone is happy. We all like to think that we're dynamite when it comes to making love. We also like to believe in our hearts that we understand the needs of our partner. But why not ask and make sure?

Once you have a handle on the previous question, I have a more important task for you to complete. Pose the following question to your better half: *"Is there anything I can do to make our love life better?"* And when he/she responds, I want you to be sensitive, open-minded, receptive, and prepared for some constructive feedback. Oftentimes, we assume that we're doing all the right things, but wouldn't you want to know if what you're doing to pleasure your partner is working...or not? Having a healthy love life isn't about your tender ego; it's about connecting on a deeper level.

Communicating to the love of your life that you're not 100% happy with your love life is a slippery slope. Defense mechanisms seem to kick in, walls can go up, and frustration can easily mount. I suggest creating an intimate moment when you're both feeling good and relaxed, then:

1. Looking for an opportunity to bring up how much you love your significant other and how committed you are to making him/her happy for years and years to come.

2. Asking your partner if he/she is mentally in a place where he or she feels comfortable talking about your love life. If the answer is yes, then proceed and be gentle in describing what you'd like to change, try next, or accomplish. If the answer is no, than respect that and ask when a better time would be, because you would like to talk about what's going on.

Mike and Sue, married for seven years, recently came to me for some communication coaching. Mike felt that Sue had lost her desire to be sexy, and consequently, their love life had significantly suffered. Sue acknowledged that their love life wasn't what it used to be, but she was still okay with it. After working with them individually, I brought them together for a face-to-face session.

Mike did an outstanding job explaining how Sue was the love of his life, the mother of his children, and that he was hers for life. But he also admitted that he felt like their love life could use a little spicing up. He made it clear that Sue was all the woman he needed, and he wanted only her. I could tell that Sue was a little on edge initially, but after she connected with Mike's positive emotional comments, she found herself agreeing that they were in a bit of a rut.

I suggested that Mike make reservations for a local getaway weekend at a hotel. They found someone to watch the kids, and Mike made dinner reservations at the hotel on Friday night, so that he and Sue could enjoy a quiet dinner, a few cocktails, and just sit and visit in the piano bar. The next day, they planned some fun activities and enjoyed some quality time alone. The phone call I got from Mike on Monday was awesome. Their weekend was a total success, and the love train for both of them was operating at full steam once again.

Don't feel comfortable talking about sex? You're not alone, but my response to you is, "Get over it!" This is your significant other I'm talking about; you should be able to tell him/her anything. What's more, by avoiding this conversation, you and your partner are never going to reach your full sexual potential. So, in essence, you're cheating yourselves! I'm not saying you won't feel vulnerable—at least initially—but trust me on this one.

• •

Telling your partner what you like (and asking him/her to share the same) can be a huge turn-on—and one of the sexiest conversations you'll ever have!

• •

Of course, there's a right and wrong way to have this conversation. For starters, it should take place outside the bedroom (you can always play "Show and Tell" later!), which is why I suggested earlier to start this dialogue during date night. That way, you're both more relaxed, there's less pressure, and you'll both feel less vulnerable. Equally important is keeping your feedback positive, so try to focus on what you like and what you want more of vs. what your partner may be doing wrong.

That said, while conducting your love life check-up, you do need to be honest and truthful. This is no time to try and sugar coat how you feel about what's going in your love life.

Ladies, keep in mind that guys will struggle much more with this process then you will. Men will sometimes downplay how they really feel about a particular issue. We'd rather run into the bathroom, stick our head in the toilet bowl and flush it over and over and over again in order to avoid any conflict and emotion. Don't let your man get away with this; even if you have to hammer on him to make him come clean.

Men, I encourage you to practice being honest. If all is well in your love life, I couldn't be happier for you. If, however, something is bothering you, or not sitting well with you, put the issue on the table for discussion.

● ●
Any topic that's on your mind and bugging you must be resolved. An unresolved issue—or issues—will begin to manifest, multiply and eventually divide your relationship.
● ●

Ladies, when engaged in a love life check-up, I encourage you to be present, and listen carefully to what your man is saying to you. Both parties need to understand the importance of not letting constructive feedback become overly personal.

How can this kind of feedback *not* be personal? It can't, but in order to expand and grow the relationship, it's your *attitude* toward the feedback that will make all the difference. For example, if I were to tell my significant other, "I wish you'd be more vocal when we make love," she could respond in one of two ways. She could get upset or offended, because maybe she thinks women who are extremely vocal in bed are less desirable and certainly not ladylike. Or, she could engage in a discussion with me and talk about how she could become more vocal.

In my current relationship, there is nothing sexier to me than when my lady talks about what we can do to bring each other more pleasure. We openly discuss what's working for each of us, as well as what could either be eliminated or improved upon. The process is amazing to me, and I'm so thankful for it.

Always remember that your partner *wants* to please you, and understanding what you like—and don't like—is the surest way to make you *both* happy. It's *your* pleasure that's on the line here, so this is always a win-win sexy conversation!

We've talked about the importance of giving and receiving, how each of us needs to find out what our partners want, and how to be honest while doing so. Now, let's tie it all together and talk about sharing fantasies. This process can be such an enjoyable journey in any relationship.

Unless you consider yourself either emotionally or sexually dead, you've likely experienced a variety of fantasies when it comes to either making love or having sex. While making love is all about connecting on an emotional level, having sex taps directly into our more carnal desires to just ravish each other. If one of these areas is out of balance, we tend to focus on what area we're lacking in, and that opens the door for both men and women to fantasize.

Men may have fantasies much more frequently, but ladies, you're in the game as well. Understanding that there is a major difference between fantasy and reality, how fun could it be for you to share— or better yet, make up—fantasies as a couple? So often this topic is taboo, and people don't want to talk about it; yet, it can play a major role in your relationship.

• •

What would you rather have: Your partner lying in bed telling you all about his/her fantasy? Or them lying in bed fantasizing about someone else?

• •

Sharing your most intimate thoughts is a bonding experience. So often we take part in behavior that accomplishes just the opposite. How you conduct your love life and thoughts about your love life can truly keep your relationship strong. By the way, fantasies vary greatly from person to person. You may have a romantic fantasy that involves candle light, good food, soft music, and gentle touching. Your partner's fantasies, on the other hand, may involve lingerie, stiletto shoes, and being playfully tied up.

• •

It's up to you and your partner to establish the guidelines. But I believe that not talking about fantasies is one of the major road blocks in relationships today.

• •

People are drawn to each other for a variety of reasons, and physical attraction is certainly a major factor. We date, we establish a physical relationship, we get engaged, and we get married. And somewhere in the process, our love life diminishes, and shortly thereafter, an emotional disconnect can occur. Before long, the relationship is in trouble, and both people are asking themselves, "How did we get here?"

Learn to communicate openly and follow the tips included in this book and I *know* you'll be happier. You chose the person you want to be with, and I want to help you get the most out of your relationship.

**CONVERSATION IS SEXY
LOVE COUPON**

"

I would love to have ten minutes of your time just to talk and to tell you how much you mean to me.

"

3

"LOOK ME IN THE EYE"

- Kiss with your eyes open
- Make love in soft light
- Fantasize about your partner
- Look into your lover's soul

D on't let the title of this book throw you off. Sexy conversation is about so much more than exchanging words. Studies show that only 30 percent of the messages we send to our loved ones revolve around what we're saying. On the flip side, a whopping 70 percent of the language of love is nonverbal! In fact, actions often speak louder than words, because nonverbal messages are perceived faster in the brain than verbal ones.

That said, here's a quick question for you: When's the last time you gazed into your significant other's eyes? If you don't recall when it was, or it's been a while, shame on you! You are robbing yourself of an amazing opportunity to experience the emotional depth of not just looking into your loved one's eyes, but into his/her soul.

Have you ever analyzed the body language of most couples when they talk? Sadly, in my observations of couples' body language, I rarely see eyes lock. Yet, not only does eye contact make partners feel closer and more connected, it's almost impossible to argue while visually engaged!

This may be one of my favorite chapters, because it's all about being visual and using your mind to create an unbreakable bond with someone you're committed to. Remember the feeling you had when you looked into your partner's eyes and realized you were falling in love? Your heart beat a little faster, your skin began to tingle, time stood still, and you felt like a teenager all over again. What an amazing moment to share with someone and a fantastic connection discovered!

The more you look into your spouse's eyes, the more you reinforce the bond you've established with him/her. It's that very sensation that I want you to experience over and over again. We sometimes forget all too quickly the closeness we enjoyed yesterday, last week, last month, or even last year, and that's why I so strongly emphasize the importance of connecting with your significant other each and every day.

When attraction turns to romance, there's a defined moment when one person steps out on a limb and delivers the message that they want the relationship to advance. For most couples, the first act of intimacy is kissing, and it can be an amazing experience. For years it's baffled me that when people kiss, most close their eyes.

- Is it just a natural reaction?
- Is it that being so close to your partner is sometimes not comfortable?
- Does it freak you out?
- Do you not like what you see?
- Does it infringe upon some unwritten law of body space?

I speak for men when I say that keeping your eyes closed while kissing does nothing but create a blank screen on the inside of your eyelids. Have you ever thought about what images fill your mind when you're kissing and your eyes are closed? What do you think about? Is there a mini-movie going on that stars someone from your past? Or did you see someone during your day that made your blood flow a little hotter? I'd wager yes, and while that movie is playing on your "screen," the person you're picturing isn't your spouse—and that's not typically healthy.

- Men tend to be more visual; thus, we will often use whatever tools we have at our disposal to get turned on. If that means creating a movie in our minds to do so, we will. The goal, ladies, is to be cast as the leading lady in that flick.

- Guys, your goal is to make your lady the star of that movie. Nothing good comes from any other image you may have in your head but that of your partner.

For these reasons, I encourage both of you to try keeping your eyes slightly open when kissing, even if for a few seconds at a time. This technique forces you to focus on your partner, be present in the moment, and enjoy the rise to passion. Peeking when you're joined at the lips allows you to see the passion in your partner, too, which can make you feel more sensual and more intimate. Gazing at your significant other also reinforces the delicious effect he/she has on you while making out, and that can be incredible. This cycle, I believe, will yield wonderful results and further draw you closer together as a couple.

● ●

Honest and open conversation leads to passion. Passion leads to making love. Making love reinforces your emotional connection, and that emotional connection keeps the lines of communication wide open. What's more, this romantic cycle just keeps repeating itself over and over.

● ●

Can something as simple as kissing with your eyes open truly have all the benefits I've mentioned? I challenge you to take the time and find out for yourself. I already have!

Now that you and your spouse are on the passion highway and moving swiftly toward an improved love life, I want you to illuminate your encounters.

● ●

Enjoy your love-making session, but don't do it in the dark! Instead, try soft light, candle light, colored light, or dim light.

● ●

If you've fallen into a pattern of making love in your bedroom with the lights off just before you go to sleep, your relationship may need a little variety added to it. I firmly believe that one of the best and most fantastic benefits that a committed relationship offers is the opportunity to have sex in an assortment of environments.

This may make you chuckle, but to me, sex and food are very similar. We all like to eat, but we all like to eat different dishes, and we all have our favorite foods. One key to a happy love life is being able to provide your partner with a sexual buffet from which to choose. Who doesn't love buffets? After all, you can go back for seconds, thirds, and fourths! So, think about serving up a smorgasbord of "tasty treats," which can begin with actions as simple as dimming—not turning off—the lights!

The key is to make sure both parties are meeting each other's physical needs, and that, as a couple, you're growing closer and more connected emotionally.

● ●
Relationships are always growing day by day. The question then becomes: "Is my relationship growing stronger or weaker?"
● ●

Other chapters in this book address how to connect physically with your partner, but if the lights are off and you can't look into your lover's eyes, the emotional connection will suffer.

Keeping the lights on also offers you the chance to *see* your lover and allows you to get turned on by him or her, instead of by some cheap fantasy. Having the lights on gives you the chance to reinforce and experience the visual of your partner as well, and what a fantastic turn on that can be!

It's been said that "The eyes are the gateway to a person's soul." At some point in your relationship, I'm sure you've looked into your significant other's eyes and felt that carnal sensation of wanting to rip his/her clothes off and ravage his or her body. At that moment, it's as if the two of you have become one, a single entity—or two souls entwined as one. In order to improve and get better at making love, you must practice, practice, and then practice some more. In order to have a happy relationship, you must achieve this cornerstone fundamental of attraction.

● ●
Find reasons to look into your spouse's eyes. Invade his or her body space. Try not to leave home without a

*hug and a glance. And while in the throes of passion,
lock eyes and share the moment together.*
● ●

Go ahead and enjoy some "window shopping" from time to time, but make your spouse the center of your attention. We live in such a promiscuous society, and each of us is bombarded by sexual images hundreds of times a day. Enjoy the views the world offers, and let them whet your appetite. But when it's comes time to eat, go home for "dinner."

Once your sexual compatibility bond has been established—or re-established—work on maintaining your sexual focus. If you find yourself thinking about or fantasizing about someone of the opposite sex, work on redirecting your focus.

The person you've committed to deserves to be the focus of your attention and the apple of your eye. Stop thinking that the grass could be greener with someone else, and work on improving your existing relationship. No partnership is perfect, but if you focus on making each day the best you can, magical things will happen between you and your soulmate. I guarantee it.

CONVERSATION IS SEXY LOVE COUPON

"

I would like to play some music, look into your eyes, and connect with you.

"

4

·~·o✖️o·~·

"BE VULNERABLE"

- You're in love; open up to your partner
- Talk about what scares you
- It's okay to show emotion
- Use jealousy to your advantage

Has someone ever looked at you and asked, "Do you need a hug?" Most people are great at being happy, but who doesn't struggle mightily when they're feeling sad or having a rough day? As your communication as a couple begins to improve, and your ability to converse deepens, you must share not only happy thoughts, but dark ones, too. Being able to connect with your significant other when your life is going great is easy, but showing your more vulnerable side by talking about topics that intimidate or scare you can be a challenge.

Men and women alike are great at showcasing their strengths. After all, that's fun to do. Who doesn't like talking about what they're good at? Pull the curtains back and take a look at someone's weaknesses, however, and you'll discover the true essence of that individual.

Can revealing your vulnerable side be scary? You bet! Where's the fun in sharing feelings of loneliness, self-consciousness, discouragement, helplessness, or insecurity? The good news is, there's an upside to being vulnerable.

When you let your defenses down, your partner sees the real you, allowing your significant other to join in and experience what's going on with you mentally. Not to mention what an amazingly freeing experience it can be when you're not afraid to be exactly who you are with someone you trust and love.

Trouble is, being vulnerable feels frightening. This is particularly true for men, who seem to channel their fears and insecurities into a corner, where they feel like they can control them. Wrong, this is very wrong! From an early age, men are conditioned to believe that exposing our weaknesses isn't masculine. Wrong again! You know that old cliché, "Two heads are better then one?" Well, as a couple, sharing lows—as well as highs—can be an amazing bonding opportunity that can super glue your connection.

What triggers feelings of vulnerability tends to vary by gender. Men, for example, feel enormous pressure to provide for their spouse and families, and they often worry if they're doing an adequate job of fulfilling those obligations. You can blame evolution for this fear. In cave men days, our sole roles were to hunt/provide food and defend our turf. Men also tend to freeze up in situations that require them to respond emotionally. Again, it's a macho thing. Being "soft" and "sensitive" makes us feel weak and less powerful—and if we reveal that side of ourselves, we fear someone might take advantage of us.

Men definitely don't like to appear stupid, which explains why, when we get lost, we are reluctant to ask for directions. I know in my past that I've been guilty of this. It's like broadcasting that we don't have a clue! Men also tend to be sexually vulnerable. After making love, we may remark, "Was that great or what?" That's because we're constantly stacking ourselves up against our significant other's former lovers—and we definitely want to feel like winners!

Women's most common vulnerabilities tend to revolve around self-image, which isn't surprising, considering how the media bombards them with toothpick-size models who wear a size zero. Many women see this and wonder, "How can I possibly measure up?" Women frequently worry about bad things happening to people they love, particularly their children. Remember, back at the cave, their primary jobs were to gather edible berries and such, as well as care for their offspring, so they evolved as super-protective. Another major fear among women is being emotionally deserted by their partner. Women have an intense desire to be fulfilled emotionally, and these needs are often met by their partners early on in a relationship. (Men tend to play along initially, because if we do, it means we'll get more sex. I know...we are such pigs sometimes!). But as time passes, their significant others may fall back into more macho patterns. And this, in turn, fuels women's vulnerabilities, because they are left feeling confused and ignored.

When it comes to vulnerability, jealousy can be a major hot button for both men and women. And if not handled right, can sabotage your relationship.

- While having dinner with her husband, a woman finds it impossible to ignore the waitress who is flirting with her significant other. Noticing that he's obviously enjoying the attention, she blurts out, "Would you rather be with her?""

- Reacting to a phone call made to his wife's office, a man may say to his spouse, "I called the office, and they told me you went to lunch with Bob again. It seems like you and Bob are getting pretty chummy."

Statements like these can fan the flame of jealousy, and there is no emotion that causes more problems—or wastes more time—between two people in a relationship. If you find yourself experiencing moderate to extreme amounts of jealousy, you need to do some deep soul searching and identify what's causing it. Jealousy breeds insecurity, and insecurity can rattle the foundation of your relationship.

Actually I think it's flattering and sexy to be proud of your spouse, and if someone of the opposite sex takes notice of him or her in a respectful manner, I believe you should turn it into a positive experience. Here are two real-life scenarios that demonstrate how to do just that...

Ladies, have you every caught your spouse engaging in what I call "window shopping?" Say you're out together in public and see him turn his head when an attractive woman walks by. For many women, the standard practice is to immediately confront their other half and make him feel as though he has just committed a crime. Often, this is followed by some snide remarks about the woman being admired: "She looks like a slut," "Those boobs are fake you know," or "I guarantee you she bleaches her hair."

• •

The comments may vary, but the intent is the same: to make your significant other feel like he's done something wrong. I disagree! Trust me, he's just being a man and responding to a visual object that caught his eye.

Just because men look at other women, it doesn't mean they want to hook up with them! And it's not meant to be disrespectful to you! By genetic code, guys simply react to visual stimuli, and when we see something we like visually, we look. Have you ever gotten on your partner's case for looking at a cool car that just drove by? I didn't think so.

So, how to turn this around and use it to help bring you closer to your spouse? Let me first remind you that your significant other is with you because he loves you. The sexy, beautiful, or classy woman he just admired can't even *begin* to compete with the bond you've already established with your man. I really need you to understand and believe that. The emotional connection you have with your partner is deeper than a quick look directed towards another woman.

●●●●●●●●●●●●●●●●●●●●●●●●●●●●●●●
Your man is with you because he loves you.
●●●●●●●●●●●●●●●●●●●●●●●●●●●●●●●

Here's a personal story that will show you what I mean. My significant other and I were out in public one afternoon, walking side-by-side, when a super sexy woman approached. Without consciously thinking about it, I noticed her. I was trying to be cool and not let my lady see that I was checking the other woman out. As most guys do, I looked at her for a few seconds and then immediately looked away as if I had never seen her. And as most guys do, I repeated this process a few more times before the attractive female passed by.

I was blown away by what happened next. Instead of feeling a shot to my ribs, or hearing, "What the hell are looking at?" my significant other remarked, "That woman was very attractive, wasn't she?" My jaw almost hit the ground, and I replied, "What did you say?" "That woman was attractive, don't you think?" she repeated.

What happened next was so amazing to me. In a split second, I had already forgotten the woman I'd admired, and my attention was instantly focused back on my partner. Not only was my focus back where it should have been, but I found myself wanting to hug my lady, grab her hand, and give her a big kiss! Did she *really* think that the woman I'd been checking out was attractive? I have no clue. What I *can* tell you is that because she didn't make me feel like a criminal, and I was able to just be a man and do a little "window shopping," I wanted to immediately find a place to make love to her. All of my energy had been transferred from the unknown woman back to my significant other in a matter of seconds—and I felt closer than ever to her.

A quick sidebar note of caution for guys: Noticing attractive women that cross your path is fine. But staring for long periods of time, and mentally "undressing" and/or "making love" to them is not okay!

Ladies, your man is going to look at other women whether you're with him or not. Acknowledge it, draw attention to it, and see how fast your man shifts his focus back to *you*. If he doesn't, it may be a sign that some walls are blocking the connection between the two of you. But if he does, as he should, watch out. You may want to prepare yourself for some passion!

Now, let's turn the tables for a minute. Guys, just as you check out other women, don't be surprised if you see other men giving your partner the once over. When you find yourself in this situation, how do you typically react? Instead of feeling threatened or jealous, I say you should be proud that others find your significant other attractive.

Keep in mind that women are so used to being pursued by men, and they have the amazing ability to block out their surroundings—to the point that they are often oblivious to guys admiring them.

And once a woman *does* notice she's being observed, she'll almost always turn to her partner and show him some type of affection.

Bask in it! And don't forget that while women do enjoy having some attention paid to them, it's the *emotional connection* they have with their partner that really touches them. Women want to reassure their significant others that they love them and only want to be with them.

Of course, if you find yourself in a situation where you're feeling jealous, you should tell your mate why you're feeling the way you are—and this holds true for both men and women. Talk about the situation, then reinforce your feelings for each other by reassuring your partner how much you love him or her, and how handsome/beautiful/hot/sexy you think he or she is. That way, you turn a potentially volatile situation into something you can both feel good about.

A couple of years ago, Sam came to me looking for help with a major jealousy problem he was having. His wife, Melissa, was a high-level executive who had to attend a lot of social events as part of her job, and Sam often joined her. When Melissa schmoozed with other men in the room, Sam's jealousy would flare up—especially when they appeared engaged in a deep conversation with his wife and would stand too close to Melissa, or would lightly touch her arm. By the end of each event, Sam would be in a terrible mood, and the two would often fight.

Once Sam was able to explain to his wife how vulnerable he felt at these events, I helped the two of them come up with a special "game" they could play that would put a positive spin on Sam's jealousy. Now, whenever Sam and Melissa are mingling and speaking to other people at social functions, both take the time to make frequent eye contact with each other from across the room. And whenever they find themselves passing or standing fairly close to each other, they make a point of touching...a brush on the arm or a quick hand squeeze. This reassures Sam that no matter who Melissa is talking to, Sam knows who she's going home with. Using this strategy has not only helped Sam overcome his feelings of jealousy, the couple has discovered that their flirtatious behavior at social events always makes them eager to get home!

Whatever your vulnerabilities are, I urge you to tear down the walls you've built to protect yourself from getting hurt, being judged, or showing weakness, and discuss your fears with your significant other. And, as each of you begins to open up, please think of every vulnerability your partner shares with you as a "gift." When you're on the receiving end, it's critical to say something along the lines of, "Thank you for sharing something so deeply personal with me." Equally important is assuring your significant other that you won't share the information with anyone else or use it in any way that could hurt or make him or her feel threatened.

It takes courage to let your guard down, but I urge you to strive for full disclosure—of the good, the bad, and the ugly. I promise you that the personal payoffs will be huge! Getting "naked" emotionally enables you to get to know—and trust—each other to the very core. Once everything is out in the open, you can work together to help and support each other, which can intensify your emotional connection. Perhaps best of all, being able to share your needs, hopes, and fears leaves you with that amazing feeling that there's at least one person on the planet that totally "gets" you. And that's sexy!

**CONVERSATION IS SEXY
LOVE COUPON**

"

*I would like to go
for a walk with
you and share
my thoughts!*

"

5

"GET OVER YOURSELF"

- Be sexy for each other
- Be critical of yourself in front of a mirror, not in the bedroom
- Bring confidence and attitude to the bedroom
- Try a little tenderness

How familiar do these phrases sound: "I'm too fat." "I'm too thin." "I'm not tall enough." "I'm not pretty enough." If you find yourself struggling with your self-image, welcome to a very large club. We *all* do it—and the overwhelming majority of us tend to be super-critical of ourselves.

Even celebrities cringe at their flaws. Tyra Banks is so insecure about her hair, that she doesn't like men to see her when she's not wearing wigs or hair extensions. Gwyneth Paltrow never thinks that she is thin enough or that her breasts are large enough. Jessica Biel longs for leaner legs, and Katy Perry frets about the acne scars on her skin.

Male celebrities appear to be slightly less vain—or at least less eager to fess up to their insecurities. Jack Black, however, has admitted that he loathes his man-boobs. Tiger Woods feels self-conscious about his calves, and, not surprisingly, Larry David and Woody Allen are insecure about, well, everything.

When I look back on relationships I've had, and speak to women about their self-image it doesn't take long before I begin to hear lines such as, "My butt is too big," "My breasts are too small," or "I don't like the way I look in the mirror when I'm naked." It is moments like these when I wish I had a police siren that I could turn on, allowing me to drown out any further attempt of this "woe-is-me" attitude. My goal would be to stop conversations like these dead in their tracks, speak loudly through the bullhorn, and exclaim, "GET OVER YOURSELF!"

• •

Here's a news flash...Most people don't like how they look in the mirror. Why do you think television airwaves bombard us daily with the latest and greatest way to trim fat and develop that six pack of abs that we long for, but most of us will never get? Exercise should definitely be a part of your life-style, but that doesn't guarantee you'll be America's Next Top Model. I encourage everyone to exercise, eat healthy, and focus on your positive attributes. All of these things will help you to be a happier person, and being happy with yourself plays a huge role in any relationship.

• •

Think about it. If you have a negative self-image, how can you can you make a positive contribution to your overall relationship?

BIG footnote: A positive self-image does *not* revolve around your physical appearance alone. We all have flaws that, given the opportunity, we would like to change. What I'm talking about here is a combination of your physical and mental characteristics.

When it comes to sexy conversation, we've already covered a lot of ground—from opening up to your partner and exposing your vulnerabilities, to kissing with your eyes open and being a good listener. Now, I want to talk to you about the importance of CONFIDENCE and ATTITUDE.

Ladies, first: Let me lay this out for you in plain and simple terms. Your significant other has chosen to be with you. He picked you for a multitude of reasons, including how you look, the things you say, and your personality.

Through the years, it continues to amaze me that the following message never seems to find its way into the female mind: "Men are suckers!" We *want* to be with you! Here's another headline: The selection process is over, and *you're* the winner. Your partner wants you, and he wants you to express yourself, and act sexy toward him.

● ●
Let me share my philosophy: Feed us, love us, be the sexy woman you are, let us spend some time with our hobby, and we'll build bridges for you. I promise!
● ●

I call this process "Sexy Sales 101." If you've ever had a sales job of any kind and can remember that internal rush you felt after making a sale, you understand what I mean. Imagine the feeling you would receive by reaching out to your spouse in a confident, sensual way and watching him respond to you as though you were a piece of fresh candy just waiting to be consumed.

Confidence equals sexy, and you don't have to be a size six with long legs and 40 DD's to pull it off. Instead, bring attitude to the bedroom— and lots of it. Every woman has positive physical features. You need to identify what yours are, then make them the focus of your sexuality. Worrying about a few extra pounds or some sagging body parts will do nothing to enhance your sex life. Self-image is something everyone struggles with, but we all have control over our attitudes. Flip the switch when it's time to make love, and be the lover your partner wants you to be. The results will amaze you!

Okay, guys, let's turn the tables and put you in the hot seat. Your challenge is to connect with your significant other on an emotional level. The last time I checked, there's no scorecard in your—or anyone else's— relationship. What I mean is, you can't wait for her to throw on a mini-skirt, high-heels, and stockings, then come rock your world. She needs to feel you are connecting with her emotionally. In the process of connecting with your partner, I have to ask you this: "Do you know what she responds to emotionally? There should be no hesitation when you answer. In order for *your* sexual tank to get filled you need to "get over yourself" and make sure *her* emotional tank is running over with an abundance of emotion.

Men are no different than women when it pertains to self-image. I don't like the way I look when I'm standing naked in front of the mirror, either. But when my significant other and I are engaged in an intimate moment, I feel like a male Hollywood sex symbol!

While men tend to be visually stimulated, remember that her hot-buttons are different. In fact, when it comes to what women find sexy in a man, study and survey results may surprise you! The good news is, you don't have to be a GQ guy with rock-hard pectorals (chest muscles) and washboard abs for your significant other to think you're hot. Nor do you have to dress in Armani suits or wear

Hugo Boss shades to impress her—although the confidence you'll feel from looking your best will help you come across as sexy.

Instead, try a little tenderness. You can never go wrong with making eye contact, which always makes women feel cherished and so special that she may melt with desire. Compliment her on the way she looks, and tell her how much she means to you—then watch her glow. Making her laugh is always a plus, too. In one survey of what women found most attractive in men, a sense of humor landed at the top of the list. Finally, sweep her off her feet by revealing your softer, more sensitive, side—and she'll find you irresistible.

What touches every woman is different, and it's up to you to find out what will get the job done with your significant other. Is it a thoughtful card with a short note telling her much you love her? A nice bouquet of her favorite flowers? Could it be letting her sleep in while you cook breakfast for her? How about a certificate to get a manicure and pedicure? Or a romantic dinner at her favorite restaurant?

Remember the old saying, "It's the thought that counts?" Show your partner that you're willing to take time out of your schedule and arrange something nice for her. Actually, I've found that it's not just the thought that counts, but the action that goes along with it. So, learn to give, and give big. The rewards will be well worth it!

One other area I want to touch on here (and will elaborate on later) is what happens in the bedroom. Again, each person has his/her own likes and dislikes, but I encourage you to be attentive to your lady, make her feel beautiful, and connect with her in a sensual way. Whether that's accomplished in foreplay, during your love-making session, or after you've reached your happy ending is up to you. Just make sure you accomplish this goal. Fill her gas tank with some emotional fuel, and she'll make your engine purr like a kitten.

CONVERSATION IS SEXY LOVE COUPON

" *Let me put on something sexy, but you can't touch me for five minutes.* "

6

"LEARN TO BE PASSIONATE"

- Love isn't always about sex
- Let the passion build
- Making love vs. having sex
- Learn to give

Most of us have been intimate with more than one partner in our lifetimes, and you probably have special memories of a particular lover and the passion that was shared between the two of you. But while the passion may have been intense and the sex memorable, it simply couldn't sustain a long-term commitment. It's wonderful to find someone that you connect with on a physical level, but what did the rest of the relationship look like? Were you compatible as a couple, or was the sex just off the hook?

Being in love isn't all about sex, but sex is definitely a part of being in love. If that sounded a little crazy and confusing, let me break it down. For a relationship to survive, a strong emotional foundation must be established.

●●
It's the rare relationship in which each person discovers they have the total package. If you've found that priceless mix of love-making and emotional stimulation, congratulations. But if you feel like your relationship needs a little work, than let's talk about the role passion and sex play in a loving relationship.
●●

Don't believe the traditional stereotypes—like women only want to cuddle and guys only want to have sex. Its often fun to joke about this with your friends, but the reality is that they are wrong.

●●
The fact is: women like to make love and have sex, and men need to connect and be invested emotionally.
●●

The question becomes, what balance will work for you and your spouse? A healthy relationship can't succeed just by making love, or just by having sex, nor can it survive based on emotion alone. When you first started dating and consummated your physical relationship, the flame of passion burned hot and wild. Late-night phone conversations, even later-night love-making sessions, were common sacrifices you were more than willing to make. You'd do anything just to be with your new lover. The adrenaline flowed, and so did the passion.

Time has a tendency to smother that flame a bit. Work schedules, kids underfoot, daily routines, and life commitments all contribute to making your once passionate love life sputter. Instead of spontaneous intimate encounters that allow you to feel wild and free, love-making has to be squeezed in where time allows. The intimate time you shared with your partner, both physically and emotionally, tends to decrease over time, and the love connection you once shared begins to suffer.

There's no outline or specific game plan I can lay out for you to solve this problem, but the issue must be dealt with.

• •

The closer you feel to your spouse on an emotional and sexual level, the more you and your partner will stay in the present and focus on the relationship. When couples begin to lose focus, outside influences gain power and chip away at the relationship's foundation.

• •

We spend more time at work than we do at home. We develop relationships with co-workers and begin to share personal, sometimes intimate, information with them. After a while, you begin to weaken the bond that's been established in your relationship and can find yourself losing focus.

• •

Be aware of how much you share with friends and family. Respect and appreciate the relationship you have. No matter what frame of mind you're in, your relationship can improve, and you can always breathe new life into it.

• •

Isn't it ironic that the very attraction that brings two individuals together can eventually drive them apart? We all remember how it felt when we first laid eyes on our significant other, and how amazing it felt to feel their touch, taste their lips, and make love until we nearly passed out. The more we made love, the more we wanted to do it again and again. But stop making love for a period of time, stop paying attention to your spouse, don't tell them all your thoughts and feelings, start taking them for granted, and the desire begins to fade.

• •

Not knowing how to communicate, letting little problems become bigger ones, failing to reach certain financial goals and not having life measure up to what you thought it would be, often leads to catastrophe. Every couple experiences changes in their relationship, both physically and mentally. The challenge is for you to grow with each other, adapt to your partner, and learn to make love all over again.

• •

Here's a heads up for guys: Research shows that it takes a man about three seconds to be interested in and ready for sex. Women, on the other hand, need about twenty minutes. For this reason, I encourage men to treat making love like a fine dining experience. Don't just rush through the salad so you can get to the main dish. Take your time and enjoy an appetizer, a sip of wine, and slowly work your way to the main course. Taste every bite and savor each moment. Most importantly, save room for dessert. Guys, we know the "happy ending" is out there waiting for us, but let the passion build with your partner.

• •

Make her feel like Cleopatra and she'll make you feel like a pharaoh. Life's problems seem trivial when you're staring into the eyes of the person you love. Just as a magician performs numerous tricks during his magic show, be magical with your spouse when it comes to being intimate. Learn what she likes, and express to her what your desires are.

• •

Ladies, men are all about passion, especially when it comes to physical passion. Over the years, I've always been entertained in conversations with women regarding men and what makes us happy. We've all heard the old cliché, "The way to a man's heart is through his stomach." In traditional relationships, that equated to the man going to work (a.k.a. cave man) and the woman spending the afternoon preparing a king's feast (a.k.a. cave woman gathering berries). The man came home to his castle, was greeted by his queen, and dinner was served. I've always believed that while that scenario worked for some, it was lacking a key element. We've established that men love food, and in my opinion, the new cliché for winning over a man should be, "The way to a man's heart is through both his stomach and his libido." That combination will open the door to your man's heart and make him feel like a king— your king. In today's world, with both women and men working full time, the traditional dinner regimen has changed. But satisfying a man's libido has not. So, ladies, ask yourself this question: "Am I giving my man the passion he needs?"

Earlier we discussed that both men and women like to make love and have sex. What balance works for you and your spouse? No matter what the ratio, it's important to balance out raw sex and making love. Sometimes the proverbial quickie gets the job done, but it's necessary to figure out a way to spend some quality time with your spouse. If you really think about it, you can break it down like this:

● ●

Hooking up for a "quickie" takes five to ten minutes. Taking time to be sensual and make love to your partner can be done in twenty to forty minutes. If I told you that all you had to do was invest forty to ninety minutes a few times a week, and you could have an incredible marriage and be the envy of all your friends, family, and co-workers, would you agree to try it?

● ●

The average person is awake for sixteen hours a day. That's 112 hours a week. Somehow, we struggle in those 112 hours to accomplish the single most important thing we can in a relationship:

making love to our significant other and reinforcing the love we share. Every couple has their own dynamic, and it's imperative that you're in tune with your spouse. We all have needs, and those needs must be met.

It would be foolish to think that a vibrant love life is the only ingredient to a successful relationship, but it is potentially the most important one. By improving communication with conversation, both parties should feel comfortable laying any and all concerns about their relationship on the table. I encourage you not to draw battle lines and not let little insignificant issues grow into bigger problems. I encourage you to work on your love life, learn to give and receive, and remember that it's much harder to be mad or frustrated with someone you just finished making love to.

We've established that sex is important and is a key ingredient when it comes to being in love. We've described the benefits of letting the passion build while being intimate, and we've talked about creating a healthy balance of making love vs. having sex.

● ●

I encourage you make time each and every day to do something nice for your spouse. You don't have to make it a competition, or top what you did the day before, but just do something to let your spouse know that you're thinking about him or her.

● ●

Yes, passion wanes, but you can always re-ignite the spark—and the intense desire you have for each other—by trying some of these strategies couples I've coached swear by:

- **Block out together time—and make it sacred.**
  Crazy schedules have a way of getting in the way of
  love and romance. When busy couples have little
  or no time to grow together, they slowly drift apart
  from each other—often without even realizing it. So,

grab your calendars and schedule some time where you can commit to giving each other your undivided attention. Take turns planning how to spend those "we" moments. Whether it's a date night, staying in for some cuddle time, or a romantic getaway on your agenda, try sending each other sexy text messages or racy e-mails the day of to say how much you're looking forward to enjoying each other's company. Building up the anticipation can lead to a better, more passionate evening.

- **Spice things up.** Routines equal ruts, especially when it comes to passion. If your favorite food is lasagna or steak, and you eat it every night, you're going to eventually get tired of it. The same is true with love and sex. You have to mix up the menu to reawaken each other's taste buds. Find ways to keep sex fresh and interesting by making love in different places, switching up your wardrobe, and experimenting with new moves and positions.

- **Take a walk down memory lane.** This is a great way to remind yourselves of how and why you fell in love in the first place. Share memories of your first impressions of one another. Recreate your first date. If you're married, flip through your wedding album. Relive your honeymoon!

- **Touch each other—a lot.** It's not called the "mother of all senses" for nothing. Studies show that physical touch sparks feelings of warmth and releases hormones that are known to rev up your sex drive.

Massages, slow dancing, making out, and taking steamy showers together are all ways to get that skin-on-skin high going for you.

- **Step out of your comfort zone.** Break out of your ho-hum routines and lose your inhibitions by trying some sexy role playing, reading erotic literature or a steamy novel together, or even watching an X-rated movie.

- **Have a sexy conversation.** Turn off the TV, pour a couple of glasses of wine, curl up on the couch, and talk—about your hopes, your dreams, your fantasies. See where the conversation leads.

Remember, it's never too late to turn up the heat in your relationship. You may have to work at love to make it last and keep it good, but imagine the fun you'll have trying to reach that goal.

**CONVERSATION IS SEXY
LOVE COUPON**

"

Please accept this invitation for a romantic evening - dinner, dancing, music, and maybe more.

"

7

"KISSING EQUALS INTIMACY"

- Start soft
- Don't be too aggressive
- Travel all over
- Whisper sweet nothings

Never underestimate the power of locking lips with your significant other. Did you know that there's an entire branch of science—called philematology—that's devoted to kissing? That's because making out offers some major benefits. Check it out...

- If you kiss your partner good-bye each morning, studies say you'll live five years longer than folks who don't do this.

• Plant a super-passionate wet one on your significant other, and you'll give about 30 facial muscles a
workout—plus you'll burn 2-3 calories a minute
(compare that to the 11 calories per minute burned
while jogging on a treadmill) *and* double your metabolic
rate. In fact, enjoy just three passionate kisses a day
(lasting at least 20 seconds each), and you'll shed an
extra pound!

• Frequent kissing is scientifically proven to stabilize
cardiovascular activity, decrease blood pressure, and
lower cholesterol.

• Think of smooching as sensual meditation.
Puckering up not only stops the "buzz" in your mind,
it also quells anxiety and heightens the experience of
being present in the moment.

• Little wonder that kissing makes us feel so happy
and euphoric. The endorphins (our body's happy
hormones) produced while making out are 200 times
more powerful than morphine!

• A passionate peck a day can keep cavities away by
preventing plaque buildup in your teeth.

• Smooching makes you high by releasing not one
but two natural stimulants: dopamine and
norepinephrine, both of which give you the same rush
you get when you try—and like—something new.

• A sweet smooch is the ultimate stress buster. That's
because it not only lowers your body's level of cortisol,
a stress hormone, it increases levels of oxytocin, an
extremely calming hormone that translates into a
feeling of peace.

This chapter is directed more to men, and if you're a female, please share this chapter with your partner. Guys, you must remember this: a kiss is more than just a kiss. Do you recall the statistic I shared with you in the previous chapter that said while you may need only 2-3 seconds to be ready to make love, a woman typically needs twenty minutes? Well, kissing is the perfect way to get her engine purring.

The problem is, as stated earlier, when it comes to intimacy and making love, men often want to experience the main course before partaking in an appetizer or two. Let's put the love-making process into a different perspective:

• •

Being intimate with your spouse is like going to watch fireworks on the Fourth of July. The show is always spectacular, but would you want the finale placed at the beginning, or would you prefer things to start slowly, build, intensify and then conclude with a big bang?

• •

If you're not already working on it, you may want to spend more time being sensual by touching and kissing your spouse. That doesn't mean jamming your tongue in her mouth for two minutes and convincing yourself that she's turned on and ready to go. Soft butterfly kisses placed strategically on her cheek, neck, lips, and shoulders can go a long way. Let your lips travel, and let them create a very sensual romantic mood.

While this section isn't meant to be a "how to" on kissing, it's important to get the point across that, unless otherwise discussed, slow and easy is better. So, take your time, and don't be in hurry. Women love to feel the emotional connection that takes place when you softly touch and kiss them. Think about it like this: During the holidays, do you aggressively rip the paper and bow off a present to see what's inside? Or do you methodically remove the bow and slowly remove the paper? Do you shove all the turkey and stuffing into your mouth and eat way too fast? Or do you chew slowly, and let your taste buds experience the bouquet of flavors?

• •
Take the extra five minutes, gentlemen, and be methodical. Will there be times when the passion flows, and both people just want to get it on? Absolutely! But a nice mix will pay off in the long run.
• •

Don't forget what we've talked about in previous chapters. Are you kissing with your eyes open? Be honest! If the answer is no, I encourage you to try it. Keeping your eyes open will keep you in the moment and focused on your significant other—and that's where your attention *should* be.

• •
Don't be in a rush as the intensity starts to build. Take some time and go exploring. Learn where your partner likes to be kissed, and take her on an adventure. Find where her sensitive spots are, and spend some time teasing her and driving her crazy. If you're interested in raising the intensity of your love-making experience, learn to be patient, and let her excitement build.
• •

Don't wait for your spouse to make you feel like a stud, either. Make her feel like a queen first. I am convinced that most men underestimate the passion that lies beneath the surface of a woman. If you're able to seduce your better half and find the combination that unlocks her womanly desires, you'll likely be blown away by the sequence of events that follows. For centuries, society has allowed men to let their sexual persona out in public, while woman are forced to act "lady like" and present a more conservative approach to day-to-day life.

• •
My wish for any man who reads this book is that he finds the volcanic passion that bubbles deep inside the woman he loves.

To accomplish that goal, you must learn to connect with her, elevate your level of communication—and most importantly, make her feel secure enough to allow herself to be completely exposed. I can't emphasize enough that making love and having sex should never become routine, or resemble a "service call." Maintain your love life, and keep adding new elements to it.

When it comes to affection, I believe that kissing is overlooked, underrated, and under-utilized as a tool of affection. If you have the opportunity to hear me give a presentation, I think you'll be entertained by how I present this topic. I've received more comments from women regarding this topic then any other.

••

To me, kissing is the key that starts the engine, and hopefully, you paid attention in mechanics school and took good notes. I've never met or spoken with a woman who doesn't appreciate a man who is a good kisser. If you're attempting to show your spouse you want to feel close to her, kissing is your ticket.

••

Since the title of this book is CONVERSATION IS SEXY, and this chapter so far has been a mini-tutorial on improving how you kiss, you may be wondering why I decided to write about this topic. While improving how you kiss is important, there is a simple tool that can be added to your arsenal that will immediately yield huge results and allow you to connect with your partner. While strategically delivering the aforementioned butterfly kisses and keeping your eyes open during the lip lock ritual, try whispering sweet nothings to your partner as well.

Describe to her how you're feeling and what you're experiencing. Tell her things like "I love you," "I want you," "You look so sexy," "I love how your body feels," "You turn me on so much," and "I love how my skin feels when it touches yours." Don't be afraid to throw gasoline on the fire and let it roar. Both sexes have their moments when raw sexual desire rules the moment, and when that happens, let the good times roll!

**CONVERSATION IS SEXY
LOVE COUPON**

"

*Let's go out for
appetizers, cocktails
and food...
Let the good
times roll!*

"

8

"PUSH THE RIGHT BUTTONS"

- Don't make assumptions
- Be electric
- Learn to massage
- Take time to tease and explore your partner's body

Have you ever been in a situation where you were sure that you knew what someone liked, only to later discover that you were way off base? It's happened to all of us at one point or another in our lives. When it comes to your love life, though, that's not a good place to be. Here are some important questions to consider:

••

Are you on the same page with your significant other?
Is there a chance you could be missing the boat when it
comes to being intimate?

••

To take full advantage of magnificent love-making moments, let me ask you this quick question: Can you list your partner's top five turn-ons? If not, you may want to go undercover and plan a romantic evening and do a little investigative work. If you find you're doing a few things wrong—or not doing others quite right—it's time to get the sexy conversation started! But be sure to keep it kind, caring, and constructive to avoid upsetting your significant other.

Many of us struggle while listening to constructive criticism. We typically get defensive and will often fire back verbally. The result is often a confrontation. Generally speaking, most people don't like confrontation, because it causes stress and can often lead to an argument.

••

Constructive criticism should never result in making
someone feel inferior or stupid. This chapter is designed
to focus on how well you know your lover and how to
learn more about him or her. My wish for you is to
make sure you're pushing the right buttons each and
every time you make love.

••

I want to pause a moment and offer some suggestions on how to reinforce positive behavior and change behaviors that you don't care for. When someone does something we don't like or care for, often our initial reaction is to confront them and immediately tell them that we don't like what they just did. In our relationships, sometimes our lovers push the right buttons, and sometimes they simply miss the mark. It's not like they're trying to do the wrong thing, so how you handle telling them can make all the difference in the world.

In my nearly two decades of playing competitive sports and training and working with men and women, I've learned that positive reinforcement is the greatest tool available in teaching. Tell me you like how I hug, and it makes me want to hug you more. Tell me you like how I kiss, and I want to kiss you more. Conversely, tell me that I'm too aggressive with my hands, and it makes me not want to touch you. Telling your lover you like what they're doing gives them the green light and confidence to repeat the behavior. Continue the positive feedback, and watch and feel how more consistent they become. And since they are focusing more on the positive behavior you have pointed out, they don't focus as much on the behavior you don't care for.   The other major benefit to this technique is that it opens the door for you to offer suggestions on what else you would like them to try or do. Here's a short list of phrases you may want to try:

- "I really like it when you do _____."
- "And I bet I'd really, really like it if you did _____."
- Or, "You really turn me on when you do _____."
- "But I have a feeling I'd be on fire if you did _____."

The bottom line is, be positive and be clear about what you like and what you would like to have happen. The results will amaze you.

If there is one thing life teaches us, it's that everybody has different likes and dislikes. The question I love to ask people is: "Do you feel that you have a good grasp on what your partner likes and dislikes?" Nobody wants to admit that they don't know their significant other well. In fact, often when I pose this question directly to couples I've coached, they'll almost always answer, "Yes, of course I know what my man/woman likes!"

•••

Let's not gamble with such an important topic. I encourage you not to make any assumptions. We all know what happens when we assume.

•••

What's more, as any relationship grows and develops, one's likes and dislikes may change. For this reason, you may want to ask yourself the following:

- "Have I stayed dialed in to my relationship's frequency?" Staying in tune with your other half as the relationship grows is incredibly important and reinforces to both parties the high level of commitment each of you has for one another.

Please understand that talking about what you like and what you want will only add to your love life and make it more enjoyable. One little tweak here, another little adaptation there, can re-establish the electrical connection in your relationship.

I also encourage you to energize your love life with some variety. Making love is about passion, emotion, and having fun. Dare I ask, "Do you still have fun making love to your partner"?

•••

So, how do you, as a couple, maintain a heightened state of erotic bliss that most couples only dream about? I know of only one way: feedback. That's right—good old down-to-earth, jump up and slap you in the face, verbal and non-verbal feedback.

•••

I've already shared with you the mind-boggling statistic that seventy percent of all communication is non-verbal. Have you ever sat in an airport and just watched people? Or sat in a restaurant observing a couple nearby having a discussion, and you just knew they were arguing? Paying attention to body language can be HUGE! Don't you want to know if your lover is happy with your performance? Since I already brought it up, don't be a baby if by some chance you stumble, or your lover let's you know that he or she is a little uncomfortable. I can't emphasize how important it is to understand how your partner communicates with you non-verbally. If you do something he's not crazy about, his body may tense up, for example. Or, a gentle nudge from her to move your hand away can be a sign of displeasure. Take nothing for granted when it comes to what pleases your significant other. Pay attention!

With the exception of now and again "quickie" sessions, making love should remind you more of starting your car in the middle of winter. Do you ever just get in, turn the key, and immediately hit the accelerator? Not if you want your car to last! Instead, you turn the car on and let it warm up for several minutes, then hit the gas. I can't say it's an absolute, but most women need to be warmed up before they hit the accelerator. This is where getting to know your spouse can be fun and connect the two of you intimately. These moments are so important, because they can help wipe away whatever pressure or worries you may be experiencing.

Find the time to enjoy the fruits and benefits of your relationship. Make foreplay a focal point of the time you spend together being intimate. This can be so much fun and intensify the love-making experience. Gentle touching and exploring your partner's entire body to find their pleasure centers should be a treat. Taking turns really helps the blood boil prior to intercourse. Play with your fingertips, and learn to use various forms of pressure to your advantage. As the passion builds, pause from time to time to build anticipation. I love this technique because I've found that it drives lovers crazy.

Are we making any progress? Understand that thresholds may vary, so learn how to tease your lover. To bring your partner to a state of frenzy, you must develop various techniques. Sometimes the animal in all of us just needs to be let out, but making love to your significant other should be more of an *event* than a quick encounter. Being physical with each other is one of the major benefits of being in a committed relationship. Don't let days and weeks pass by before you look back and find it hard to remember the last time that you and your spouse shared some intimate time.

If the above process isn't happening quite the way you'd like it to, try giving your partner a massage. Most people really enjoy the attention and guys, I'm not just talking about you. Women love to feel special, so I encourage you to learn the art of massage. Not only is it a fantastic tool to help you relax, it can also be a major turn-on and help get you where you want to go. It's not time consuming; in fact, it can be done in five or ten minutes—about the amount of time it took to warm up that cold engine in the middle of winter.

Once you've hit the gas and find yourselves cruising down love's highway, remember that it's always a smart move to check in periodically with your lover to make sure that all the buttons you're pushing are the right ones.

CONVERSATION IS SEXY
LOVE COUPON

"

Let's go lingerie shopping, and I will cook dinner for two in my new outfit.

"

9

"Turn Off The TV"

- Direct attention to your partner and family
- Music is a turn on
- Dance with your partner
- Let the good times roll

It's amazing to me that couples invest so much time in dating, getting to know each other, developing a long-term relationship, and making the commitment to be together in a monogamous capacity. Yet, most fail to establish a few, if any, relationship guidelines. In a matter of months, couples begin to develop daily routines that are counterproductive to bonding and growing closer together. We spend a great deal of time working (not really an option), taking care of personal business, spending time with family, and supporting our life-styles.

Here's an eye-opener: According to one recent study, most of us spend more time commuting back and forth to work and watching TV than we do alone with our significant others!

> *We sometimes forget to set aside time every day to invest in our relationship. Your relationship operates in similar fashion to a bank account. When you invest time, energy, and thought, it's like making a deposit. Let's refer to the account as an emotional asset. The other side of the equation, however, works just the opposite. Every day that goes by and you don't invest time, energy, and thought, you're making a withdrawal.*

It's not uncommon to arrive home from work, execute a quick change of clothes, turn on the TV, and zone out. How much television do we watch? According to a recent Nielsen study, the average American watches approximately 153 hours of TV a month. That's five hours a day, on average!

Everyone needs the chance to exhale and figure out the best way to make the transition from work mode to relationship/family mode. But we must do a better job of this if our relationships are going to be successful. Ask yourself this question at the end of each day: "Did I make a deposit or a withdrawal in my relationship account today?"

• •

As an alternative to your daily routine, consider the following: What would your family time be like if, instead of turning on the TV, you turned on the radio, or popped in a CD that everyone could enjoy listening to? This may sound a bit out of the ordinary in your household, but I assure you that the results will be impressive.

• •

Why do people come home and immediately turn on the TV? I call it *distraction without interaction*. You're in the same room as your spouse, but are you really paying attention to him or her? No! Sure, you may both comment on what's happening, and conversation fills the air, but there's no real interaction. And don't try to tell me that you turn on the TV just to catch up on the day's news.

Nice try. Through the internet and conversations with friends and co-workers, the news of the day is absorbed before you ever get home. Other than a quick update on tomorrow's weather, what's on the boob tube that you really need to see? TV is a great way to pass time and to avoid actually talking to those around you. Republicans will always disagree with Democrats, and no matter who's in the White House, they're always going to be criticized. Sure, once in a while, there's a blockbuster news event that demands our attention, but for the most part, television has become nothing but a distraction that takes time away from our personal lives. Turn some music on instead, and talk to each other. The interaction will promote a stronger couple and family bond.

Once upon a time, conversation and interaction between family members was a common occurrence. They would sit down to eat with no blaring television in sight. What typically happened next? Conversation would break out! Siblings would talk to each other, kids would speak to their parents, and parents would even talk to one another.

● ●

CONVERSATION IS SEXY is all about highlighting the positive effects con-versation can have on the people you have relationships with. It's not just about men and women, but learning to speak and communicate with your children. Sometimes it seems like people find more reasons not to talk to each other instead of learning how to communicate.

● ●

Music is a great conversation tool that takes you back in time, brings back sweet memories, and reminds you of special events in your life. We all have songs that we associate with certain periods and events in our lives. Those songs make us feel and experience those emotions all over again. Need proof that what I'm saying is true?

● ●

When's the last time you were driving in your car, and a song came on that you immediately identified with? Perhaps it was a favorite tune from your high school or college days. Or maybe it was a love song that reminded you of when you and your significant other first met and fell in love. Within seconds, you were likely singing along at the top of your lungs, and it made you feel happy. We all have songs that trigger flashbacks in the form of a mental slide show.

● ●

Music is powerful, and even if you and your partner have different tastes, you can always find a genre or even a few artists that you both like. So, tune it in, turn it up and the let the music turn you on. Better yet, how about putting some music on and dancing with your partner? What a great way to bond and connect!

● ●

Music feeds the soul and makes us feel good, so grab your partner once in a while and ask him or her to dance. You'll love the results.

● ●

Music encourages and allows you to experience raw emotion. What a wonderful experience that can be, and I urge you to seek out opportunities that make you feel that way. In essence we all have songs, hobbies, or activities that make us feel happy and amazing. If you've ever seen the movie *Happy Gilmore*, a comedy that stars Adam Sandler, there's a line in the movie when one of the characters tells Happy Gilmore to "find his 'happy place.'" Whatever exists for you in your happy place is where you'll find the raw emotion I'm speaking about.

A significant danger zone in any relationship centers on people looking for ways to deflect emotion. Watching excessive amounts of television, talking about the neighbors' marital problems, gossiping with friends, or being overly critical of co-workers are all activities and behaviors that people typically use to deflect emotion. Those behaviors can be poison to your relationship, and you need to avoid getting caught up in them. Please take a second and absorb the previous sentence.

• •
I can't emphasize enough how much time and energy people waste by talking about everyone else's problems and misfortunes instead of focusing and directing attention towards their own relationship. Is this a quest to make our life seem less chaotic then other people's lives? I truly feel that too many people look for ways to make their own lives seem better than others.
• •

I encourage you to search for and find ways to focus on your partner. You have no bigger fan, no stauncher ally, and no better friend. How your relationship grows and matures will be determined by the two of you. Some people say that relationships are hard work, and while that opinion carries an element of truth, I believe that the right relationship should be fun.

Speaking of fun, it's really important to focus on having way more of it as a couple. Every couple knows instinctively that their relationships are happier when they make time for fun. Unfortunately, fun is often the first activity to fall by the wayside as life's other demands pile up. Don't let that be the case in your relationship. Recent research conducted at the University of Denver's Center for Marital and Family Studies revealed that finding moments to be playful together is not just an indulgence...it's a necessity. In fact, the correlation between relationship happiness and having fun is significant—and sky high. So, go ahead and whip up a romantic dinner together, go exploring at a local flea market, or challenge each other to a friendly game of HORSE on a nearby basketball court. And yes, you can even snuggle up together once a week and watch a favorite TV show together, especially if it revolves around another couple in love, and watching it could spark interesting—and sexy—conversations between the two of you afterwards.

In other words, eliminate distractive behaviors, and replace them with interactive ones, then sit back and enjoy the ride. Have dinner, clean up the dishes, put the kids to bed, put on some Barry White (he's a personal favorite of mine), look at your significant other and ask, "May I have this dance?"

CONVERSATION IS SEXY
LOVE COUPON

" *Would you slow dance with me tonight? You pick the song!* "

10

"Shop Together"

- Pick out clothes together
- Tell your partner what he/she looks good in
- Ladies, be a diva!
- Make shopping romantic

Guys, do you like your significant other to look beautiful, smell sensual, and dress sexy? I'm going to go out on limb and say the answer to all the former questions is a big "Yes!" Ladies, do you get turned on when you see your man looking good in a tight pair of jeans, or dressed up in the style he looks best in? Again, my crystal ball tells me yes. Both sexes can have what they want, but to get to that point, you're going to have to do some shopping.

> *Most women love to shop; men, not so much. But maybe it's time you guys stepped up to take one for the team. Before your testosterone meter bends over backwards and you think I've lost my mind, roll with me for a minute.*

Shopping with the woman you love presents an opportunity for you to take part in an activity that she may enjoy. It's also a great way to spend some quality time together *and* rack up relationship points you can cash in on down the road. And did I mention that when one or both of you later wears something you picked out and purchased together, it can bring back memories of good times—which could very well lead to an unexpected evening of romance and passion?

Men and women alike want to look good and find clothes that make them feel good. So why not go along with your spouse and use this opportunity to bond? Ladies, I know there are times when shopping with your gal pals can be more of a social get-together, but shopping with your spouse can be fun, too.

● ●
Most guys reading this may be laughing at the notion that shopping can be fun, because their previous experiences have been negative. Let's turn that around. After all, shopping for dish towels or shower curtains isn't really much fun, but shopping for clothes your partner looks super sexy in can be a whole other experience.
● ●

In fact, I encourage you to not only go along for the ride, but to learn how to be an active and supportive participant. To make your joint shopping experience pleasurable, however, you need a game plan..

Instead of just blindly heading to the mall, or wherever you decide to shop, decide on the number of stores you're comfortable visiting or agree on a time frame. That way, you'll avoid the anxiety buildup men tend to get when it comes to shopping, and they won't be rolling their eyes, glancing at their watch, or muttering phrases like, "Come on already" or "I'd like to make it back home before the game starts."

Ladies, I also recommend that you do a little bit of homework first. Flip through fashion magazines or circulars for stores you plan to visit to get an idea of the kind of clothes you're interested in trying on. Studies show that one of women's top complaints about men when they shop together is that she feels rushed or pressured. But by scoping things out ahead of time, you can narrow your choices and will be able to make faster decisions while still enjoying the experience.

Try to involve your partner in this step by asking for his input. For example, his eye may be drawn to a certain outfit from your favorite magazine, and he might say, "Wow, you would look awesome in that!" On the flip side, he may spot an outfit and remark, "I'm not crazy about that color" or "That's not sexy to me at all." The goal here is not only to engage your man and get him to take stock in what you wear, but to get him excited about watching you try on outfits that he already *knows* he likes. Remember, we men are visual creatures.

Before heading out on a shopping spree, it's always a good idea to talk finances and to set a spending limit—or at least, pick a range you're both comfortable with. You don't want your shopping excursion to be ruined by a financial feud.

Once you're out and about, be aware of—and respect—gender differences in shopping. Remember, men tend to be "hunters". When something catches their eye, they just want to spear it and take it home. Women, on the other hand, tend to be "gatherers". They prefer to graze and browse.

Guys, once your significant other begins trying on outfits for you, sit back and enjoy the show! Be ready to answer questions like, "The red one or the black one?" or, "Does this outfit make me look good?". And don't even think about responding with, "Whatever you like best, honey." She is asking you because she wants your support and affirmation. Guys, this is your chance to interact with her and tell her what you like to see her in—and what you think makes her look good.

Keep in mind that when trying on clothes, women will often test the waters and make comments like, "I don't look good in this," or "This makes me look fat," or "My butt is too big." Be compassionate and complimentary of her, as this is a very sensitive process for most women. She may not be a top model prospect, but your significant other needs to feel like she's *exactly* that—and the job of communicating that message to her is yours. Don't expect to be wowed by every outfit she models for you, but definitely show enthusiasm for the ones you do like. Tell her that she looks amazingly sexy in something that catches your eye—then watch her face light up with an appreciative smile.

• •

Ladies, you need to be open, supportive and encourage feedback from your partner. Become the diva that he wants you to be. Be the woman your man will always fantasize about. As the saying goes, "Sex sells," so put your man in a buying frenzy. Make the experience fun and enjoyable, and you'll have much more success at getting him to go shopping with you again in the future.

• •

Ladies, this may surprise you, but helping your significant other shop for clothes can be fun, too, and he could probably really use your help. Studies show that when men shop, they tend to do so aimlessly. That's because they are linear thinkers. This means they typically go into a store with a set plan: get in, get what they need, get out. And when they can't find what they want? Most men would rather bail than flag down a salesperson. Remember, for many men, asking for help implies weakness.

Men may not be as fashion conscious as women are, but we do like to look good for the woman we love. So, step up and be our personal shoppers! Help us make a list of what we need ahead of time so we can shop commando style, which is our preferred way to go. And once we start trying things on, tell us how handsome or hot we look when you see something you like.

• •

For most men, shopping is like going to the dentist and finding out they need to have at least two teeth pulled. So ladies, I urge you to have some patience and allow this process to grow and develop. Start slow and make the first few excursions relatively brief.

• •

Keep the overall shopping experience positive. Don't be afraid to break up your outing with a nice lunch break—and be sure to treat yourselves to something decadent.

Speaking of decadent, don't limit your shopping experience to casual, work, and dress-up wear. If there's a Victoria's Secret—or similar store—wherever you're going, and you walk by without going in, I'll be ashamed of you! Shopping for women's lingerie together can take your experience to a whole new level. Need I say more?

While shopping, always pay attention to each other's body language, and if things start to turn negative, talk it out and decide whether it would be best to continue shopping or call it a day.

I hope after reading this that you've both created a movie in your mind depicting how this process could play out and make you feel closer and more connected. I hope I've also convinced you that shopping together can be romantic. But don't just take my word for it. According to a recent survey, seventy-four percent of men and women said they shopped together so they could spend more quality time together. Seventy-five percent said they always hold hands when they shop. And forty-six percent admitted to kissing and other displays of affection while shopping together. I say go for it—and shop till you drop!

**CONVERSATION IS SEXY
LOVE COUPON**

"

*I want to take
you on a shopping
spree at the store
of your choice!*

"

11

"VICTORIA'S SECRET, AND THEN SOME"

- It's okay to play
- Lingerie rocks
- Compliment her
- Fuel the Fire

I love this chapter and could spend hours talking about the possibilities, effects, and benefits of lingerie in or out of the bedroom. You might say that's just because I'm a man, but here's the thing...

••

Lingerie is sexy, seductive, erotic and great for everyone's self esteem.

••

Granted, for men, sexy lingerie is like "unwrapping" a present. We know that removing that wrapping and being able to play with what's underneath will make us happy and satisfied. But guess what? Lingerie can put a skip in *her* step, too! For women, wearing something slinky and sexy is a major confidence booster. When she looks sexy, she feels sexy, and she becomes sexy—often shedding inhibitions and unleashing passions she may otherwise feel timid about.

Lingerie is also a win-win for your relationship. Men, being men, are fascinated by visuals and instantly create powerfully stimulating images in their mind when they see their significant other wearing something lacy or racy. Women, on the other hand, love with their brain and crave an emotional connection. They want to be assured that their mate finds them desirable and sexy. Well, watching their partner salivate over what they're wearing can certainly do the trick. So, with lingerie, both men and women get what they need for great sex *and* a deeper emotional connection.

Victoria's Secret hasn't become a multimillion dollar company just because women need to wear bras and underwear. It's all about the sizzle of sex, and I hope that every couple reading this book embraces this concept. Women want to be viewed as sexy, and men want their women to look and act sexy. Victoria's Secret brought lingerie into mainstream America and made men feel good about going into a women's store to shop for their significant others.

● ●

There is something magical about the carnal chemistry that takes place between a man and woman in that moment when the door swings open, or she walks around the corner and reveals her sexy outfit for the evening. It may only stay on for seconds, or minutes, but what a rush it causes.

● ●

It doesn't matter whether your comfort level is a simple teddy with spaghetti straps, a corset, a garter belt and a pair of stockings, or thigh-high riding boots. It's up to you and your spouse to talk about what kick-starts your love life. The bottom line is, lingerie sends the message to your spouse that its time to connect and spend some quality time together. Ladies, don't be afraid to be spontaneous and excuse yourself from the room, then moments later, invite your man to join you in the bedroom for some hugging, touching, and love-making. Making love is a fifty-fifty split, and guys love it when their partner takes the initiative to step up and show that she wants him *right now*.

• •

Men love to be wanted, and there's no better way to send that message than by surprising him with some new lingerie. When he sees you, he'll know exactly what you have in mind. And he'll be especially appreciative that he's the only one invited to this private showing/ unveiling.

• •

Day-to-day problems and hassles at work can make it hard to put the business of the day behind you and switch gears to relationship-building mode. Establish a routine when you get home that allows you a few minutes to exhale the day away and inhale the evening that lies ahead. You may only have a few hours to spend together before heading off to sleep, but you need to make them count.

• •

Don't let the day dictate what happens in your relationship. Work is mandatory, and the kids have to be taken care of, but there are twenty-four hours in a day. I suggest you spend at least a half hour of quality time every day with your partner—and watching TV doesn't count! Before the lights go out, and each of you heads off to sleep, pause and ask yourselves this question: "Did we connect today?" Some nights, the gas tank may be empty, but if its not, rev up your engines and go racing.

• •

Guys, don't be afraid to communicate to your partner that you're feeling frisky and would love to see her put on something a little more enticing and sexy. And ladies, if you're in the mood to be seduced, play along! Seeing you in sexy lingerie allows men to visually separate you from the many other roles you play in life—at work, as a wife, as a mother. Slip on something sexy, and he'll get the message loud and clear that your favorite role—at least for the moment—is as his lover.

Guys, when your significant other does take the time to dress in something provocative, you need to take the time to compliment her on how beautiful and sexy she looks. As tempting as it may be, try not to get caught up in the moment and just rip her clothes off to get to the good stuff.

• •
Make her feel special for making the effort. Positive reinforcement is very powerful and rewarding. Make it a goal each and every day to make her feel special— even when making love is not on your agenda.
• •

A constant theme you'll notice in this book centers around "effort". If you are always waiting for your partner to compliment you first, congratulate you first, acknowledge your hard work first, or do something special for you first, then your relationship is in trouble. Effort is all about taking the bull by the horns. I love it when my significant other comes up and touches or kisses me, when she compliments me regarding something I've done, or tells me she thinks I'm handsome. Even if I'm in a negative mindset, she can change it in a heartbeat—and then I feel my blood start to flow.

• •
Because she does that for me, it makes me want to do the same for her. This process takes a little more work for men, but it has to be a goal. I've always believed

*that in any relationship, you are either growing closer
together, or you are growing apart.*

Lay down a foundation of positive and loving behaviors with your partner that make you grow together and feel closer to each other. We all have our own likes, dislikes, hobbies, and favorite past times. Sifting through those can really help you bond with your better half. Taking a walk, listening to music, exercising, or eating a quiet meal together are all behaviors that can keep you growing together.

● ●
*Having individual time is both healthy and important,
too. Just make sure it maintains that status and doesn't
become a negative. For example, I love to play golf, but
I'm sure doing it both Saturday and Sunday might cause
a little tension in my relationship. So, go ahead and
enjoy time with the boys, or a girls' night out, but make
sure that both of you are on board with what's going
on.*
● ●

Connecting is all about feeling appreciated, wanted, sexy, and desirable. With the divorce rate in America over fifty percent, it's clear that over the course of days, weeks, months and years, we can lose focus on how to grow together in a relationship.

● ●
*As humans, we seem to spend more time focusing on
all the negative things going on in our lives, and we pay
little attention to the positive aspects of our lives.*
● ●

Credit card bills, the house or rent payment, the kids, a car payment, or how much money you have to live on until you get paid again are all issues that can easily dominate our minds. All of these thoughts can weigh on a person's mental state, and before you know it, it's time to go to bed and hope that tomorrow will be a little better.

I encourage you to spend time together each and every day. Do you remember the last time you looked into each other's eyes and felt the tingling feeling of your spouse's fingers touching you?

If you want to lose weight, you have to work at it. It's probable that you'll have to change a few of your eating habits as well. If you want to tone up your muscles, you have work out at the gym. Well, guess what? Love also needs to be exercised on a regular basis. Neglect it, and it becomes soft and weak. But exercise your love, and it will blossom and grow.

●●●●●●●●●●●●●●●●●●●●●●●●●●●

●●●●●●●●●●●●●●●●●●●●●●●●●●●

**CONVERSATION IS SEXY
LOVE COUPON**

"

*This coupon
entitles you
to a gift
certificate at
Victoria's Secret.*

"

12

-~෴෴-

"No Boundaries"

- What happens in your bedroom is private
- Continue to grow
- When things go awry, get help
- Take the bull by the horns

As your connection as a couple deepens, and you begin to experience a new level of intimacy, your love life will soar to new heights. This provides you and your significant other with the opportunity to express any and all thoughts you have about what you'd like to change when it comes to making love. Embrace the importance of communicating the type of love life you want with your spouse. If you believe that relationships grow over time—and I assure you that they do—then so must your love life. What those boundaries are can only be determined and decided between you and your partner.

I'm sure you've heard the popular phrase pertaining to Las Vegas: "What happens in Vegas stays in Vegas." Well, I'd like you to apply the same concept—with a slight twist—to your love life.

●●●
Whatever happens in your bedroom should stay in your bedroom. There is nothing more sacred in a relationship than what takes place behind closed doors. Cherish your love life, but protect and keep it private, too.
●●●

I caution the men reading this book to heed the following: I can't tell you how many conversations I've been involved in over the past twenty-five years, where guys will offer private details of their love life. Play-by-play disclosure of events, places, and sexual acts are discussed with pride. As these tales of various adventures intensify, testosterone levels rise. But in many instances, I've also seen these conversations come back to bite guys in the rear end. People love to gossip, and private information such as this is gold.

●●●
Take pride in your love life, but keep what happens between the sheets under cover. Brag about the positive aspects of what goes on in the bedroom, but don't be suckered into detailed conversation where you may reveal too many secrets. Kiss, but don't tell.
●●●

Communicating openly is what this book is all about. This process not only involves having the ability to tell your spouse what's on your mind, but being able to hear what your spouse is saying to you as well. Communication is a two-way street, but all too often we find ourselves on a one-way dead end.

• •

Hidden thoughts and fantasies can poison even the best of relationships. Left in the closet and kept from your significant other, I assure you that they will someday come out to haunt you.

• •

CONVERSATION IS SEXY, and expressing your deepest desires to the one you love is an amazing turn-on. *There should be no secrets!* How you make love, the type of language you use to communicate, what type of clothes you wear, and where you decide to be intimate are all topics that need to be discussed. Probe and find out what really excites and pleases your significant other. Understanding what your other half likes and dislikes can unlock his/her "emotional safe." Find out how to bond with your significant other on the deepest level of intimacy, and you'll have a partner for life.

One big reason I'm so adamant about this topic is because, all too often, men and women allow life's stresses to dictate and interrupt their love lives. At some point in a relationship, it becomes natural for women to feel less attractive to their spouse, and for men to feel less wanted. More time passes, and you both become disconnected from each other. Before you know it, the last thing you want to do is be intimate with your significant other. You find yourself watching more TV, doing more yard work, or spending more time with family and friends.

• •

Communication disconnects lead to a divided relationship, and that can often lead to divorce.

• •

When a disconnection lasts for a given period of time, neither person feels special to the other anymore. One or both of you may start casting your fishing line out to see what's swimming out in the ocean of attention. Cast enough times, and eventually you'll hook something. I think you can see where I'm going with this.

• •

If your relationship has reached the point where you get a rush from talking to other women or men, I urge you to monitor the situation and keep it in check. All relationships experience peaks and valleys, and we tend to be most vulnerable when we are in an emotional valley. There are many reasons that cause us to feel a bit down, but that's a time when both men and women tend to make mistakes that can sometimes be fatal to their committed relationships.

• •

If you've become discouraged in your relationship and have thoughts about getting divorced, I would encourage you to seek professional help. Remember, "The grass isn't always greener on the other side." The fairy tale image that exists regarding marriage or long-term relationships is often just that—a fairy tale.

• •

Since humans aren't perfect, it seems logical to conclude that our relationships aren't perfect.

• •

Seeing a professional before a crisis develops can truly get you back on the right track and save your relationship. There are no absolutes in life, and I understand that some couples should not be together. But if you loved your spouse when you got married, and after a certain period of time found out that you've lost that love along the way, I believe you can get it back. Will it take some time, commitment, and hard work? Absolutely, but it can be done—and, in fact, I've seen it happen in many, many couples I've coached.

• •

Let me be clear: No matter how bad your relationship is, the process of divorce is not fun. Having been there, done that myself, there is no way to describe the pain, loneliness, and despair associated with a divorce. I have no clue what the process feels like for women, but to me, I wouldn't wish the lonely days and dark nights on my worst enemy. If there is any hope left in your marriage, I encourage you to use this book, and whatever other resources you have, to try to figure out a way to reconnect and save your relationship. For some of you reading this, you may feel your marriage has reached a point of no return, and there's simply no saving it. After digesting this book and getting counsel from family, friends, and professionals, you may choose to use this book as the foundation of success for that special person waiting out there for you. I believe in love, I believe there's no greater gift than emotional connection, and I believe each of us can have it.

• •

Let me remove the dark cloud hanging over this conversation and tell you that by using the chapters in this book to revive or improve your relationship, I firmly believe that you can achieve great things.

• •

Take the bull by the horns and start improving communication with your significant other today. Take the bull by the horns and understand that keeping your spouse focused on your relationship directly relates to how satisfied he or she is with you and your love life. Take the bull by the horns and connect with your spouse regarding his or her desires.

• •

Find time each and every day to talk, touch, hug, massage, kiss or make love. Make time to bond daily with your partner and to tell him/her how you can't imagine living without them. Remember, CONVERSATION IS SEXY and Affection equals Connection. So, go look your partner in the eye, say, "I love you," and plant a big old, open-eyed kiss on his or her lips.

Better yet, make a daily habit of incorporating loving gestures like this in your routine, and the connection between you will know no boundaries.

**CONVERSATION IS SEXY
LOVE COUPON**

"

*Your wish is
my command.
This coupon
entitles you to
two hours of
my services.*

"

13

"HISTORY : LEARN FROM THE PAST"

- History is a great teacher
- Learn from your mistakes
- Make positive changes
- Set a new course for the future

There is a prevailing theory among many scholars that states: "In order to succeed, one must experience failure first." While that doesn't sound overly enticing to most of us, it turns out this theory rings true. Growing up, how many kids did you know who jumped on a bicycle for the first time and just took off down the street shouting, "Look at me, Mom!" or "Look at me, Dad!"

Most of us left several layers of skin on the ground before finally figuring out how to balance ourselves and keep the bike upright. Once we learned how to pedal that two-wheeled machine, we never forgot; hence, another cliché: "It's as easy as riding a bike." The point is, riding a bike becomes easy after learning to distribute and balance your weight properly. Even if you don't get on one for a few years, you can still climb aboard and go for a ride.

When it comes to relationships, we're always trying to figure out how to get on our "bike," distribute our weight, and ride off into the sunset. We keep getting on, then falling off, getting on, and falling off. And for some of us, it becomes a pattern that plays out over and over and over— just like a broken record or a CD with a scratch on it. So, the question becomes: "How do we become more successful in relationships, and more importantly, in our current relationship?" I believe one answer is: History! Not very sexy, I know. Yet, history is one of the greatest teachers we have, and for some reason, many of us don't do a very good job of paying closer attention to it.

At one time or another, the greatest minds and inventors in the world have relied on history to help teach, guide, and create new opportunities. In many instances, those who've tried before us and failed, have saved us the pain and heartache of repeating their mistakes. But we've all also had our own fair share of stumbles— and learned valuable lessons while picking up the pieces. The combination of our past experiences and learning from other experienced relationship veterans are great tools that can help you avoid potential pitfalls. Relationships are no different than going to school—there are always new lessons to be learned. So, do your homework and pay attention in "class" everyday.

From the time we entered puberty, we boys began to realize that the thought of holding a girl's hand really wasn't going to make us throw up. For girls, boys were suddenly no longer gross and disgusting; in fact, it felt good to interact with them. The learning curve had begun.

During adolescence, new romances burned hot and fast and eventually, they fizzled—usually over silly reasons. Maybe she said something mean to you, or maybe he spilled a secret about you to his best friend. The end result was that you learned something. When your first "serious" boyfriend or girlfriend came along, you were so "in love" and couldn't stand being apart—until you spotted your best friend making out with him/her. Again, you learned something. Finally, the first time you told your significant other that you'd be home for dinner at seven, but showed up two hours later—half drunk—I'm sure you learned something then, too.

We all have the greatest opportunity to learn from our mistakes, whatever they may be. Just like presents come in all sizes, shapes, forms, and varieties, so do our screw-ups. The key is learning to use these in a positive manner. Hopefully, you have the ability to be honest with yourself and own up to the mistakes you've made in the past. It's not the most enjoyable process you can put yourself through, but as a learning tool, it's priceless. Our past is our history, and as we gain experience in relationships, it's paramount that we do not forget both the positive and negative events of those relationships.

I get it that you'd much rather forget the bad times. Who wouldn't? But I believe it's crucial that you embrace those memories, because you can learn so much from them. As I've already pointed out, relationships take two people to make them succeed, and it takes two people to make them fail. What's important to you as an individual—man or woman—is to take inventory of what role you played when things were positive, as well as what role you played when things were not so positive.

• •
This is so important, because what the sciences have taught us regarding behavior is this: Left unattended and ignored, behavior patterns will repeat themselves over and over again.
• •

If you're always ten minutes late and you're okay with that, then you'll probably always be ten minutes late. If you're not a very affectionate person, and nobody comes into your life and shows you the benefits of being affectionate, you'll likely never adopt that manner of expressing yourself. I use this specific example for a very good reason. As a kid, I remember my dad as being larger than life—and not just because he was six-foot-three, weighed about 250 lbs, and was a great athlete. His mom and dad were not very affectionate to each other, and I can remember my mom telling me how hard she had to work at getting him to show affection to me and my four siblings. My mom would constantly remind him to hug and kiss us when we went to bed. And when he seemed reluctant to do this, she'd often tell me that he was simply afraid of hugging us too hard, or he worried that if he picked us up, he might drop us.

Turns out, that was all smoke and mirrors. Later in life, mom told me that dad just didn't feel comfortable showing affection to us kids, having not received much of it from his own parents. Nevertheless, my mom was relentless at getting him to hug and kiss us, and over time, he did change. This story is so on point with this chapter, because when asked to describe my dad, I would tell you this: "He was the kindest and most loving father a son could ever ask for." I remember my dad hugging me every night before I went to bed, and even when he came home from work. Up until his passing, I hugged him every time I went to visit, and again when I left.

My dad's family was important enough to him that he stepped out of his comfort zone and changed his conditioned behavior pattern to help build a stronger bond with his kids. Here was a man born in 1928, who lived through the Great Depression, who enlisted in the Army for two years at age eighteen so he could get the G.I. Bill to go to college, who completed his college education, got married in 1954, and fathered five children. If *he* could change his behavior, then maybe you can, too.

We all have behavior patterns—some good and some not so good—that can manifest into problems in our relationships. You need to identify yours, address them, and design a plan to change the not so positive ones.

Step 1: Make Your List

Here's an exercise I'd like you to do, and I promise that the results will be worth your effort. Get out a pen and paper, and draw a line down the middle to make two columns. At the top of the left-hand column, write, "Positive Behaviors". At the top of the right-hand column, write "Not So Positive Behaviors". Now, take five minutes (and please time yourself) to write down five behavior patterns that you see in yourself and view as positive. Examples might be that you're a clean person and keep your belongings organized, that you always remember important dates like birthdays and anniversaries, or that you hug your spouse whenever you see him or her. As you make your list, give it some solid thought.

Done? Now take five minutes and make a list of the not-so-positive behaviors, or patterns, you've noticed about yourself. Examples might be that you're not a very punctual person, that you're sloppy around the house, that you spend too much time with your friends, or that you're not a very patient person.

Don't over think this. You may smoke too much, drink too much, procrastinate, talk too much, or be a bad listener. We all have faults, and it's time to get yours on paper. Don't hesitate to ask your family, friends, and loved ones to give you their opinion. I always love getting outside feedback when it comes to what my friends and family feel are my strong and not-so-strong points.

STOP

Now that you've taken the time to identify which of your behaviors are positive and which are not, we can get some work done. I want to start with what you wrote in the top right-hand column. It's a good idea to be alone when you do this and understand that it's critical to be honest with yourself. With nobody around, there's no excuse to hide from the truth. Think of this as a real growth opportunity. If you embrace this process, the results could be life changing.

Taking into consideration your current relationship—as well as any past serious relationships—I want you to re-read the behaviors you listed that aren't so positive, and then take some time to reflect and ask yourself: "Did any of my not-so-positive behaviors have an effect on my relationships?"

In essence, did any of the behaviors you listed either contribute to or lead to the end of any of your relationships? If so, place a mark by that particular behavior. I encourage you to devote a significant amount of time to this step, as the more time you spend, the more you'll learn about yourself. There's no question that relationships are complex, and why a particular relationship didn't work out can be challenging to analyze. What's paramount to you—and your future success in relationships—is to identify your "relationship strengths," as I like to call them, as well as your "relationship challenges."

Upon conclusion of this exercise, you should have a few—or maybe several—check marks next to one or more behaviors that affected your past relationships—and maybe even your current one. This is HUGE! You now have on paper, staring you right in the face, the areas you struggle with and the potential causes of why your relationship (or relationships) have struggled.

• •

Some behavior patterns are more easily dealt with than others. Always leaving your dirty underwear or socks on the floor can be irritating over time, and maybe even cause a few heated discussions with your significant other. But rarely is this a deal breaker in most relationships. This behavior can be more easily changed

*than if you have a problem with drugs, alcohol, or anger. Remember, other than chemical dependency, **all behavior is learned**. And the best part about learned behavior is that it can be unlearned—if you're willing to make the commitment and effort to change.*
● ●

Once you've identified what behaviors are causing problems for you, or what behavior patterns are eating away at your relationship, you can begin to address them. Please understand that, depending on the behaviors you want to change, this process can take some time, and you may even need to seek professional counseling to help you.

Step 2: Design and Construct
a Plan that will Yield Results

Depending on what behavior(s) you're trying to change, this step can be relatively easy—or it can be the challenge of a lifetime. For instance, admitting that you use too much profanity in your daily speech pattern is great, but you may have to include friends, family, and loved ones to help you alter this behavior. Whatever not-so-positive behavior patterns you're trying to tackle, I encourage you to include your inner circle of friends and family in this step of the process. Don't think you have to change behavioral patterns on your own. Those who love you are always willing to assist you. I've not only utilized this process successfully myself, I have seen others do it, too, and achieve amazing results.

Using the above example, imagine telling those around you that you're trying to cut profanity out of your daily speech pattern, and every time you say something inappropriate, you want them to bring it to your attention. Within a few days, you should experience a significant change in this bothersome behavior. Granted, while a behavior pattern such as not using profanity can typically be changed in a short period of time, other behavior patterns may take longer.

The key is to have your list available, look at it everyday, and have a plan of attack ready on how to make the change.

Step 3: Eat an Elephant

If you've taken this process to heart and really made an effort to focus on things you want to change, I believe you can make it happen. Think of it in these terms: If you can make little shifts in your behavior every day—and I'm talking baby steps—you can achieve huge results. Remember, Rome wasn't built in a day, but string enough days together and the city finally rose.

A college football coach I once knew described to me his philosophy on building a championship team. He told me that becoming a National Champion was like eating an elephant: You just have do it one bite at a time. I had the privilege of standing next to him after his team accomplished their goal, and what an amazing feat it was. I utilize his philosophy to this day, and I can tell you it works. The process is easy:

1. Be honest with yourself.
2. Identify what you'd like to change.
3. Design a plan on how to accomplish the goal.
4. Take a bite out of the elephant every day.
5. Celebrate the results.

Before wrapping up this chapter, I want you to go back to your list and read the behaviors you wrote down in the left hand column. Those behaviors or patterns are your strengths. Read them aloud, and allow yourself to feel good about them. Reinforce—and celebrate—the great things you do on a daily basis that give strength not only to your relationship, but to your life. All too often, we don't take the time to acknowledge the positive aspects of our personalities and lives. This isn't some crazy cheerleading session—it's just a reminder to focus on what you like about yourself, and then go attack the changes you're committed to making.

Improving your current relationship—or having more success in your next relationship—is within your reach, but it's critical that you take a hard look in the mirror and try every day to be a better husband/wife, father/mother, girlfriend/boyfriend. The people in your life will not only notice the effort, they'll love you for it.

CONVERSATION IS SEXY
LOVE COUPON

"

Let's turn back
the clock -

This entitles you to
a weekend getaway
at a destination
of your choice.

"

14

·-~᷑᷑᷑᷑᷑~·-

"BE TOLERANT AND LEARN TO FORGIVE"

- Tolerance and forgiveness equal success
- We all make mistakes
- Love means having to say you're sorry
- Clear the air and move on

In one corner, we have the mad-as-hell husband, wearing a scowl, shaking his head in disbelief, and muttering to himself, "How could she do this?" He has just glanced at the couple's checking account statement and discovered that his spouse went on a shopping spree after recently losing her job. In the other corner, we have the wife, tight-lipped and wearing a look of defiance. Instead of explaining that she needed clothes to wear to job interviews, she's opted to pout and give her spouse the silent treatment

I am often asked, "What makes a relationship work?" The answer is threefold: communication, tolerance, and forgiveness. I firmly believe that those three components are what make a relationship successful. Since the theme of this book so far has been communication, I believe we should all be on the same page at this point. So, let's talk about how being tolerant and forgiving is priceless—as well as how both can be difficult to achieve, no matter how much in love you are.

I opened this chapter with a boxing analogy for a reason. Oftentimes, when one partner or the other messes up, instead of discussing what happened, both head for their respective corners to fume or sulk. Or, the gloves go on and fighting ensues. Either way, nothing gets solved, and nobody learns from the experience.

I believe this happens because we are all, more or less, socialized to be "selfish." Before becoming part of a couple, we're busy blazing trails as individuals—finding jobs for ourselves, managing our own finances and households, fulfilling our own needs, and protecting ourselves. Who else will do this for us? Then, once "he and she" become "we", and things go awry or tough decisions need to be made, that "looking-out-for-number-one" mentality kicks in. It happens almost automatically—sort of like a default button.

Truth is, nobody's perfect, everyone screws up, and we all have our little quirks, idiosyncrasies, and annoying habits that can drive our significant others insane. Ignore all of this, and you'll be amazed at how quickly walls of resentment go up. Find ways to discuss and deal with these issues, however, and you'll be equally amazed at how quickly those walls can come tumbling down.

Your inside voice may have already told you how compassionate you are, and that you're already a very tolerant and forgiving person. Let's check it out! We've all developed a certain set of standards when it comes to tolerance and forgiveness. Suppose someone pulls out in front of you while driving home from work. While it may irritate you for a few seconds, you probably shrug it off and quickly forget about it. Five minutes later, the same situation occurs, and you immediately sense your blood beginning to boil. Still, you find a way to let it go. Within seconds, another driver nearly misses hitting you, cuts you off, and causes you to slam on your brakes. Now you've had it! The expletives start to fly, you gesture the one-finger salute, and you find yourself screaming at the top of your lungs.

What happened to tolerance and forgiveness? Let me be clear, I dislike battling traffic and bad drivers as much as anyone. I grew up minutes outside of Washington D.C. and not only had to negotiate the downtown streets, but the Capital Beltway itself. My heart goes out to all commuters nationwide. The point is, most people view forgiveness based on our level of tolerance. We can forgive friends, family members, and loved ones for just about anything—as long as it's inside our tolerance boundaries.

What's the difference between tolerance and forgiveness? Actually, the two are closely related, but not quite the same. To explain the distinction, allow me to go off on a short tangent about tolerance.

To me, tolerance is more about putting up with the small, everyday stuff your spouse does (or doesn't do) that irritates you. These can run the gamut:

- Leaving the cap off the toothpaste tube
- Leaving the toilet seat up
- Dropping dirty clothes on the floor
- Leaving dirty dishes in the sink
- Driving too fast (or too slow)
- Being consistently late
- Letting the house get too messy

These may seem like petty grievances and hardly a reason to get worked up about, but the fact is, little annoyances, if not dealt with, can chisel away at your relationship.

How to deal with each other's weird little tics? It's always a good idea to start a conversation about what's bugging you. If you bury it, you risk feeling resentment, and, over time, that can drive a wedge in your relationship. Don't nag. Don't yell. And definitely don't give ultimatums. Just calmly bring up the annoying behavior, explain why it bothers you, and see if your significant other is open to changing this particular habit.

It may not happen! Some habits are difficult—if not impossible—to change, or your partner may give you the "accept-me-for-who-I-am-and-deal-with-it" attitude. If that's the case, you need to decide whether the issue is trivial enough to tolerate, or whether it's worth arguing about. In other words, pick your battles—and remember that most annoying habits are not worth getting bent out of shape over.

Always try to focus on the bigger picture by thinking of all your significant other's good qualities instead, and hopefully, that will help you go from rolling your eyes to wanting to kiss him or her for being so awesome overall.

Don't take it personally. Your partner doesn't mean to annoy you or hurt your feelings when he consistently forgets to roll the trash can to the curb on Tuesday morning, or when she forgot to buy your favorite kind of toilet paper again. And above all, accept the fact that your significant other probably has a list of things *you* do that get on his or her nerves, too!

Petty annoyances don't typically require or involve forgiveness. That's reserved for bigger issues. Again, nobody's perfect. In fact, we all do dumb things each and every day of our lives. Some of our careless behaviors or actions are relatively minor in nature and can be put into the "no big deal" category. But sooner or later, we all stumble and fall flat on our faces.

• •

Forgiving someone for being thirty minutes late for dinner is one thing. Going on a shopping spree for a new set of living room furniture, or buying a new set of golf clubs when the joint bank account is empty, however, can cause World War III.

• •

Within seconds of committing a ridiculous or inappropriate behavior, our minds begin telling us "I just screwed up." And if our mistake involves or affects our relationship, the very next thought sprinting through our minds is typically, "I hope he/she will forgive me."

• •

It's easy to idealize the person we cherish most, but the fact is, we all make mistakes, and we all need forgiveness at some point in our lives.

• •

It may sound a bit cliché, but do you believe in second chances? Has anyone ever forgiven you for acting inappropriately? Have you ever been given a second chance by anyone? I imagine the answer to at least one of these questions would be yes! In marriage and long-term relationships, the stakes are higher, but the concept remains the same. Forgiveness opens the door to growth.

• •

Studies show that couples who forgive each other are happier than those who don't—and that happy couples are also quicker to forgive one another.

• •

Forgiving your partner when you've been hurt, let down, disappointed, or wronged, isn't easy, but the benefits of letting your significant other off the hook are huge. For starters, scientists say forgiveness makes you happier and healthier. It's good for your heart—literally—in that it lowers heart rate and blood pressure, plus it decreases stress. When you forgive, you'll sleep better, since letting go of a grudge can bring you peace and closure. You'll feel less anxious, too, since you'll no longer feel the need to obsess over how upset or angry you are.

In fact, think of forgiveness as a gift you give to *yourself.* Suppose, for example, that your significant other takes his or her mother's side in a major disagreement you were having with her. That can hurt, and you've probably earned the right to stew about it for a little while. But eventually, you need to ask yourself, "Am I really willing to waste any more time and energy on this matter?" Hopefully, your answer will be, "No!"

● ●

Before you say, "I forgive you," be sure to talk to your significant other about the behavior that upset you. It's almost impossible to forgive until you feel heard and understood. Part of living together is adapting to each other and defining behavioral guidelines that work for both of you.

● ●

What about when you're the offender? There's a right way to ask for forgiveness. First, you need to swallow your pride, admit you were wrong, and take responsibility for your actions. No excuses! Second, you need to offer your significant other a genuine, heartfelt apology. Next, you need to find a way to make amends, by asking "What can I do to make it up to you?" You caused the problem— now find a way to be part of the solution. Finally, reassure your partner that it won't happen again, or that you'll do better next time. Otherwise, you're not likely to be so easily forgiven. Surely you've heard that saying, "First time, shame on you; second time, shame on me!"

● ●

Remember, your partner's forgiveness is not the same thing as condoning what you've done. He or she is not saying, "Oh, that's okay...why not do it again?" So, don't treat forgiveness as a "hall pass" to continue acting inappropriately.

• •

Once the two of you have cleared the air, it's time to take action, it's time to move on.

• •

Learn to forgive and then talk about the situation. Orchestrate a game plan to deal with the behavior so it stops being a problem.

• •

Before you can move on and get back to the business of growing together as a couple, you need to discuss the offending behavior and make plans on how to keep it from occurring again. Having this conversation will help you rebuild trust and open the door to moving forward.

• •

If you're always five minutes late, try setting your watch or clocks ten minutes fast. If you forget things easily, get a programmable device and train yourself to use it. If your financial situation is out of balance, communicate and take steps to make a plan on how to improve it.

• •

Of course, there are major issues that can affect your relationship where forgiveness is harder to come by. The most common example: What if you discover that your other half has been unfaithful? I know this is a tough one, but I urge you not to make any snap decisions. Oftentimes, there are layers and layers of issues that need to be addressed and dealt with, and one-on-one and/or couples counseling can help. I only hope you can work through the problems and reconnect.

Hopefully, moving forward can be accomplished together as a couple, but sometimes it means saying good-bye.

●●●

There are couples who have survived everything from total financial loss to infidelity. Others in the same situation have buckled and looked to place blame, assign accountability and/or demanded to know, "How could you have done this to me, or us?" Both men and women have either heard or said this at some point in their relationship.

●●●

While I don't condone destructive behaviors in any relationship, I've come to realize that such behaviors are usually a symptom or symptoms of other problems. Alcoholism, drug addiction, gambling addictions and other compulsive behaviors are diseases and require immediate professional attention. Paying attention to someone of the opposite sex above and beyond normal interaction is often a symptom that something isn't right at home.

That's why I'm so focused on communication. Remember how we've talked about how good we humans are at letting little problems become really big ones? Small, seemingly insignificant, issues can build and contribute to that ever-dreadful emotional disconnect. So, learn to deal with the little problems, and you'll have fewer actions to forgive—or beg forgiveness for!

Perhaps the best part about forgiveness is that it restores positive feelings and behaviors in your relationship. Once the air has cleared and valuable lessons have been learned, it also instills a sense of pride—"Hey, we survived this...we're invincible!"

**CONVERSATION IS SEXY
LOVE COUPON**

"

I want to reconnect with you. Let's clear the air and make a plan for the future. I want to be yours forever.

"

15

"THE LANGUAGE OF LOVE"

- Words are gold
- Speak with passion
- Ignite the fire
- End on a positive

I remember struggling academically in high school. I wasn't the worst student in my class, but never did I threaten to make a run for class valedictorian. While math, history and P.E. were my favorite classes, English was a class I merely tolerated—barely. I think it's safe to say that I would rather have been dragged across asphalt than attend English class, and yes, I get the irony of that situation now, thank you! But all of that changed during my senior year, when we began reading the works of guy from a few centuries back named William Shakespeare.

I understand that not everyone is a fan, and no, I don't have a copy of *Romeo & Juliet* on my nightstand. But as I began to read his works and figure out his style, I found myself connecting with what he was saying.

For the first time in my life, I began to realize that words, when put together in the right order, can be not only descriptive, but penetrating. I challenge you to think of a movie you like or a song that makes you feel happy, and the reason it's one of your favorites centers around the words being used to deliver the message. Depending on the era you grew up in and the type of movies you love, a line such as "Frankly my dear, I don't give damn," is immediately recognized from *Gone With The Wind* when Rhett Butler is speaking to Scarlet O'Hara. How about when Martin Luther King delivered the opening line of his now historic "I Have a Dream" speech from the steps of the Lincoln Memorial? Or, how about the line, "Rose if you jump, I jump. Do you hear me Rose?" from the Academy Award winner, *Titanic*?

The bottom line is, words are gold, and put in the right sequence and said at the right time, they pack a mighty punch. Shakespeare opened my eyes and mind and showed me how powerful they can be. Unfortunately, all too often words are used in a negative way and not used enough to offer support, show compassion, and express positive feelings. We teach our young to use their words to express themselves instead of screaming or crying. And yet, as adults, we sometimes forget their power.

Why is it that we don't use words in a more positive way? Think back to the look on one of your co-worker's faces the last time you told him or her, "Good job!" or "Thanks for helping me out." Do you remember how you felt the last time someone said something positive to you? The feedback is both immediate and impactful. If you want to make someone's day tomorrow, give him or her a compliment. Tell him he looks great in that new suit, or tell her she looks awesome in yellow.

If a few kind words can put a smile on the face of someone you work with or someone you hardly know, imagine the impact they can have on the person you love and spend everyday with! Todd's Theory number 247 (that was supposed to be funny) is: Practice speaking with passion about the things in your life you're passionate about! Ask a musician to talk about music, and they'll go on for hours. Ask parents to talk about their kids, and you'll usually get an earful updating you on everything from how little Johnny is doing in school to how he's a force on his Little League baseball team. Ask people to talk about their number one passion, and you won't be able to shut them up. Yet, when a couple is struggling in their marriage you'll often hear them say, "We just don't communicate well anymore." My question is, "Did you ever?"

I've found in my travels, in conversations with couples I coach, and among folks who attend my seminars, that we can all use some help in learning how to speak with passion. What's more, when it comes to the person you're committed to, shouldn't you be speaking with passion to him/her on a daily basis?

Saying, "I love you, honey" as you're walking out the door is a nice little bone to throw out. But what would happen if you spiced it up just a bit? Instead of shouting it on the way out the door, suppose you walked up to her, put your lips next to her ear, and whispered, "I love you, and I can't wait to see you when I get home tonight." My guess is that you'll get a much different reaction!

Remember, we talked about the importance of connecting on a daily basis, and more importantly, connecting in the morning and at night. Life throws so many distractions our way, and for whatever reason, our minds seem to allow this to happen. It just takes a little focus each day to make the person you're with feel special, wanted, and appreciated. Yeah, I know everyone has a bad day once in a while. I do, too. But keeping your eye on the prize may not be as hard as you think.

In the previous example I had the man engage his significant other by whispering in her ear and making her skin tingle just a little. Ladies, your goal here is no different. Men love to be enticed and tantalized. I sometimes refer to this as the "Come-and-get-it" objective, and let me explain. Men get excited when they know something good is coming down the road, but it's just not quite here yet. I love using food as an example to drive this point home. Most people have a favorite food or meal that just makes their mouth water. For me, its filet mignon, a baked potato with butter, and a dinner salad, followed by something with hot fudge for dessert. Man, that's good! When I know that's on tap for dinner, my mind goes wild, and I can't wait to cut into that steak, plunge into that baked potato, and devour that hot fudge whatever it is—and I don't care, because I know it's going to taste so good. The salad is okay...hey, you need to get your veggies somewhere.

Where am I going with this? Ladies, make *yourself* his favorite meal to come home to. Make your significant other feel good about leaving work, running his errands, getting his gym workout in—or whatever he does at the end of his day. But give him a positive reason to get his butt home.

With today's modern technology of email, texting, video chatting or whatever else you do to communicate, there's no excuse not to connect every day. A simple text message that says, "I love you," "I miss you," or "I can't wait to see you later" can go a long way in keeping your connection super strong.

Since we're talking about the language of love, don't hesitate to whet your significant other's appetite with just the right words. Have you ever noticed how certain words just feel good when you say them—like delicious (I love that word) or gorgeous? Guys, if you ever want to see a woman glow and smile ear-to-ear, tell her that she looks gorgeous or even delicious. If you think I'm crazy, try it!

Stop a woman you think is attractive, and tell her she looks gorgeous, and watch her reaction. Then imagine what the reaction would be from your significant other. It may sound a bit corny, but we all *want* affirmation from our partner, we crave it and we *need* it. I love the rush I feel when people special to me take the time to send me a message or call to tell me they love me.

I know we've talked about how women are generally more emotionally based, and men are more sexually based. Still, I truly believe that both men and women not only enjoy, but want to hear that they're appreciated, wanted, and loved. Men can put up the biggest macho front they want, but find a creative way to tell them you can't wait to see them and exchange some kind of affection, and they will love it—admit it or not.

Language and words are fantastic tools to ignite the fire in your love life. Every couple establishes their own verbal boundaries and guidelines. I'm not going to offer any great words or lines to use when you're in the throes of passion, because what may work for one couple would be a total disaster for another. What I encourage you to do, however is be creative with words and develop your own language of love. Try talking more when you make love. Find out what words or phrases your partner enjoys hearing, and most importantly, mix it up and find new words to bring some sizzle into your bedroom. Words can help fill up a woman's emotional tank, and they can unleash the "Tarzan" component of just about any man's inner self. You don't need to wax poetically or stoop to levels you're not comfortable with. But if you want to keep your relationship bond in tact, you must use your language of love to keep things right where they should be. Take time every day and send a message to the love of your life to let them know how much he/she means to you.

One of the greatest joys I believe life has to offer us is the ability to climb in bed at night and wake up the next morning next to the person you love. If you're not starting your day and ending it on a positive note, you're simply missing out on the opportunity to give that special someone right next to you the affirmation he/she needs to either sleep tight or attack the day. As humans, we don't do so well when we're alone, and I truly believe that my day is always a little brighter knowing I'm not going through it alone. Whispering a quick "Love you, babe" as you roll over and turn out the lights is one way to wrap up the day. But remember CONVERSATION IS SEXY, and getting a little more creative with what you say can linger longer in the mind of your loved one and make him or her feel so incredibly special.

CONVERSATION IS SEXY
LOVE COUPON

"

Let's light some candles, put on some music, and create our own love-making fantasy.

"

BONUS COUPONS

**CONVERSATION IS SEXY
LOVE COUPON**

"

Let's go somewhere quiet, tear down any walls that have built up, and enjoy each other. I love you and want you to be happy.

"

**CONVERSATION IS SEXY
LOVE COUPON**

" *This coupon entitles you to a fifteen minute massage followed by a passionate kissing session.* "

**CONVERSATION IS SEXY
LOVE COUPON**

"

*Please go out
with me this
weekend so I
can show you
off to everyone.*

"

CONVERSATION IS SEXY
LOVE COUPON

"

I'd like to take
you out to lunch
and then give
you some
'afternoon delight.'

"

**CONVERSATION IS SEXY
LOVE COUPON**

"

Let's put some music on, and I will give you a neck rub.

"

**CONVERSATION IS SEXY
LOVE COUPON**

"

*I'll be your
GENIE tonight -
I grant you
ONE wish!*

"

CONVERSATION IS SEXY
LOVE COUPON

FREE Admission
for ONE to a
"Conversation is Sexy"
Seminar.
Register at
www.conversationissexy.com

THE *CONVERSATION IS SEXY*
SEMINAR SERIES - AND MORE

Todd Reed's services include personal communication coaching (both for individuals and couples), keynote speeches, and seminars. Here's a small sampling of seminar topics. Coach Todd also welcomes the opportunity to customize a seminar specifically for your group.

CRACKING THE GENDER CODE

Are men really from Mars and women from Venus? Absolutely! Gender differences affect almost every aspect of our lives—from the boardroom to the bedroom. They explain why so much can get "lost in translation" when you and your significant other communicate, as well as why either or both of you can often feel misunderstood—and disconnected. In this seminar, Coach Todd will:

- Explain why men and women tend to be motivated by different things and have different needs
- Share the (often) hidden messages behind what "he says" and "she says"
- Crack the gender code so that you can *finally* understand not only what makes each other tick, but what turns each other on
- Show you how embracing your differences can propel you to new levels of understanding—and intimacy

GET IN THE GAME

If you want to hit a grand slam in the game of love, communicating with your significant other is key. In this seminar, Coach Todd provides tips and techniques that will show you how to:

- Be a team player to keep your relationship strong and solid
- Use verbal and nonverbal communication to be a cleanup hitter
- Dodge communication pitfalls so you never have to play Monday morning quarterback
- Pinch hit when you've stumbled
- Up the ante in the romance department

THE BUFFET OF LOVE

It would be foolish to think that a vibrant love life is the only ingredient to a successful relationship, but it is potentially the most important one. This seminar offers a smorgasbord of tips on how to spice up your love life, including:

- How mixing up the menu can reawaken your taste buds
- Why "appetizers" should always be on the menu.
- How music can work wonders: tune it in, turn it up, and let it turn you on
- Why you should always save room for "dessert"

LOVE AND ROMANCE: THE AHA FACTOR

Conversation is Sexy is chock full of "light bulb" moments that can help you rediscover the joy and fun of being in a committed relationship. In this seminar, Coach Todd will have you saying, "Wow, I never realized that!" over and over again by sharing "aha" moments that include how:

- Kissing with your eyes open can pump up the passion in your relationship
- Jealousy can bring you closer together
- A simple text message or email exchange can lead to a passionate evening
- Being vulnerable side can take your relationship to a whole new level
- Replacing "I love you, babe" with a more creative phrase can rev up your romance tenfold
- Men need only 2-3 seconds, but women typically require 20 minutes to get "in the mood"

THE LANGUAGE OF LOVE

Language and words are fantastic tools to ignite the fire in your love life. But remember, too, that actions often speak louder than words. This seminar covers the important roles both verbal and nonverbal cues play in keeping the love lines of communication flowing in a relationship, including how:

- Simple statements and gestures like these can make your significant other feel heard—and understood
- Locking eyes can create an unbreakable bond
- Asking the right questions can keep your love tank filled
- Tapping into the "mother of all senses" can send sparks flying
- Talking more when you make love can bring more into your bedroom

For more information, contact Coach Todd at
www.conversationissexy.com
(406) 396-7755

www.ingramcontent.com/pod-product-compliance
Lightning Source LLC
Chambersburg PA
CBHW021334090426
42742CB00008B/598